BENTLEY and BENTLEY CONTINENTAL CARS

ISBN 978-1-84155-594-2

CONTENTS

Model:
MARK VI 4½ LITRE

Maker:
BENTLEY MOTORS
(1931) LTD.
14-15 Conduit Street, London, W.1

IN AN introduction to the Bentley catalogue, Raymond Mays says that whilst he wouldn't claim the Bentley to be unique in its ability to be driven flat out from dawn to dark, it does take such treatment without the ghost of a hint that it *might* register expensive rebellion. "Peace of mind of that order naturally costs money," says Mr. Mays, and he has had no hesitation in using his standard Bentley for unofficial road practice over the racing circuits of Europe—a gruelling test, indeed, for a car that combines a high performance with the highest degree of comfort and luxury.

Since 1951, a revised design of engine has been fitted to the Bentley chassis, the capacity being raised to 4.56 litres. Other detail modifications were also made to the power unit and these have increased the performance throughout the speed range. With overhead inlet and side exhaust valves in an aluminium head, this design provides maximum power with the minimum length of engine.

Interesting chassis details of the Bentley Mark VI include independent front wheel suspension with coil springs and wishbones supplemented by an anti-roll bar. Spring damping is controllable through adjustable shock absorbers with a ride-control lever on the steering wheel. The transmission has been re-designed and the centre propeller shaft bearing is supported by a controlled flexible mounting of patented design which eliminates all traces of vibration.

Since the war, the Bentley has been offered by the makers with a standard four-door sports saloon body of all-steel construction manufactured by Bentley Motors. Offering luxurious accommodation for five persons and with very full equipment, the standard Bentley saloon retains the traditional radiator with the razor-edge style of coachwork.

Recent modifications include a re-styling of the body, offering increased luggage accommodation which now totals 17½ cu. ft. The overall length of the car has been increased by 7½ ins., and a change has been made in the body moulding. Other relatively minor modifications to increase performance and comfort have also been incorporated in the latest edition of the standard Bentley Saloon.

Other bodywork styles include a four-door sports saloon by H. J. Mulliner, a drophead foursome coupé by Park Ward, a two-door sports saloon by James Young and a similar type of layout by Park Ward.

A new addition to the Bentley range, for limited production for export only, is a 120 m.p.h. streamlined saloon of lighter weight and increased power, The close-coupled body is by H. J. Mulliner, Ltd.

INTERIOR
Four-door Sports Saloon .

FOUR-DOOR SPORTS SALOON

Engine
Cylinders	.. ..	6
Capacity	.. ..	4,566 cc.
Bore ..	.. .. ..	92 mm.
Stroke	.. .. ..	114 mm.
Valves	Overhead inlet, side exhaust	
Compression Ratio	.. ..	6.4:1
R.A.C. Rating	.. .. ..	31.5 h.p.

Transmission
Clutch .. 11 inch Single dry plate (semi-centrifugal)

Gearbox .. .. .. Four speeds fwd.
Control .. Right-hand change on R/H drive. Steering column on L/H drive.

Overall Ratios:
Top	.. ..	3.7
Third	.. ..	5.0
Second	.. ..	7.5
First	.. ..	11.11
Rear Axle ..	.. ..	Hypoid Bevel

Suspension
Front Independent coil spring and wishbone
Rear .. .. Semi-elliptic leaf springs

Brakes .. .. Mechanically servo assisted

Dimensions
Wheelbase ..	.. ..	..10 ft. 0 ins.
Track	.. .. (front)	4 ft. 8½ ins.
	(rear)	4 ft. 10½ ins.
Tyre Size ..	.. .. ..	6.50—16

Performance
Approx. Petrol Consumption .. 17 m.p.g.
Fuel Tank Capacity .. .. 18 galls.

Prices
Model: Four door sports saloon by Bentley Motors (1931) Ltd.
Basic £3,100 plus P.T. Total £4,823 14s. 5d.

Model: Four-door Sports Saloon by H. J. Mulliner & Co. Ltd.
Basic £4,190 plus P.T. Total £6,519 5s. 7d.

Model: Drophead Foursome Coupé by Park Ward & Co. Ltd.
Basic £4,280 plus P.T. Total £6,659 5s. 7d.

Model: Two-door Sports Saloon by James Young Ltd.
Basic £4,280 plus P.T. Total £6,659 5s. 7d.

distinctive Bentley vintage era

An exceptional eight-litre that started life as a Red Label in 1924, and for a time was supercharged: a Speed Six that has seen the world; and a four-and-a-half of 1936 vintage—aren't they all in greater or lesser degree cars of distinction? Every keen driver of a Cricklewood-made, or "W.O.", Bentley would say that this is the case; and examination of the machines on view at any of the Bentley Drivers' Club gatherings at Silverstone, Hyde Park or elsewhere gives weight to that view. They were a wonderful breed, and happily a goodly percentage of the considerable number still on the road are in splendid condition and for the most part "as originally turned out". Unfortunately, some have been altered and, for the true appreciator, ruined by various changes and botchings that are too painful to contemplate or write about. That fate, of course, is by no means confined to Bentleys; but it always seems more outrageous—to us—when this sort of thing is done to a noble thoroughbred. A lesser machine can carry it, somehow—albeit rather pathetically.

Not all the great old-type Bentleys, however, are splendidly-maintained, strictly-as-catalogued specimens. Like others with vintage interest, we confess to leaning toward the side of the purists. We like to see, for instance, a nicely-kept three-litre Vanden Plas wearing its original long sweeping wings and short running boards—or well-made, and expensive no doubt, replicas of these absolutely right "setters-off" of that most handsome of all sporting tourer bodies. Not for us the non-original helmet-type wings; or the P100 or other lamps that were never fitted to these cars when new. Non-rubber rear lamps can, however, be forgiven!

Be that as it may, and with utter illogicality, we are with the majority when we walk around the Lycett eight-litre. Indignation, real or simulated? Never! Without question that fine car is a Bentley of Bentleys, something better than W.O. had time to conceive as the sands of the old firm were running out. We are certain, anyway, that he approved of what the late Forrest Lycett and McKenzie evolved to such purpose. That great car has fortunately passed into good hands. Its general specification and exactly-right appearance are too well known to call for attention here; and its performance is, of course, a legend.

One of the greatest

Another "special" Bentley we have always greatly admired is John L. Goddard's handsome and potent machine. The pictures herewith attest to its good looks and as for perform-

Mr. Goddard's 8-litre Bentley competing at Blandford hill-climb and looking anything but cumbersome

Magnificent powerhouse: the large six-cylinder engine of the 8-litre is handsomely simple in the true Vintage tradition

The other Bentley six-cylinder of the era: the Speed-six. This is the engine installed in Mr. Jupe's car during restoration

ance, that is in the exclusive very top bracket for "real" Bentleys. One illustration will suffice. In May of last year the Antwerp Motor Union arranged a meeting on the motor-road outside Antwerp, the section being closed for the timing of standing and flying kilometre runs. Ten members of the Bentley Drivers' Club took part and Mr. Goddard was easily the fastest of the Bentleys, which included Mr. Stanley Sedgwick's R-type Continental sandwiched among the representative bunch of vintage Bentleys. The Goddard 3/8-litre covered the standing distance (mean of runs in both directions) in 28.13 seconds and registered a mean speed for the flying kilo of no less than 136.149 mph. This was second fastest time of the day, a 250 GT Ferrari being the only modern car to beat the Bentley. Batten's 8-litre Bentley returned a speed of over 121 mph and the well-known 3/4½-litre of G.H.G. Burton 116.242 mph. The best 3-litre (W.F.J. Brogden's) slightly bettered a mean speed of 89 mph.

Mr. Goddard is in Australia at the moment although his well-known Bentley (pictured here in combat with the formidable Lycett car/driver combination) is garaged near London, under the care of Donald McKenzie. Obviously, however, his Bentley data are with him, for he promptly sent us some interesting notes from Sydney. He wrote: HT 9029 started life in 1924 as a single-carbie (Smith's multi-jet) Red Label 3-litre. Body, an open four-seater Vanden Plas, was painted brown. The car was purchased from Henly's of Great Portland Street in 1928, for £350. with around 80,000 on the clock. In 1929 the engine was supercharged by adding a Cozette blower and carburetter, giving 4½ lb of boost. The blower drive was taken from the after end of the camshaft, the ratio was 3 to 1 and it was gear driven. The firm of ENV made the pinions and fitted the wheels on their tapers. Lubrication was by jet at the point of gear teeth contact, bled off the main supply and returned by gravity to the crankcase. The installation of the blower and modification to the car, etc., was carried out by Wadham Bros, of Southampton, under the quite superlative supervision of their foreman, Harry Penn; the work was done by Les Smith, who was at that time their leading fitter.

The result of this modification was very gratifying. Maximum speed rose from 80 to 95 mph, and providing the car was driven with an eye on the boost gauge so that this was kept as near to zero as possible, the fuel consumption decreased from 17 to 20 miles to the gallon. At no time, no matter how hard the driving, did it get below 16.

In 1930, Mr. Goddard's notes continued, I was lucky enough to pick up a standard Bentley six-cylinder car for £70, and it was this engine that was installed in HT 9029 after being brought up to Speed Six specification by Bentley Motors' service station at Kingsbury Lane under the eagle eye of Ivermeah. (He later went to Bristol's and did the development work on the Bristol BMW-based engine.)

After the war I found an 8-litre languishing in a junk yard outside Salisbury. No-one was interested as the engine number was of the YR series, which indicated that the crankcase was of the earlier, not stiffened type. I bought it for £100, sold the tyres and P100 lights for £50, and got "Mac" (Senior), much against his will, to strip the engine. Great was the surprise when it was discovered that the crankcase had the thickened webs for stiffening the main bearings.

Mac now changed his tune, sold me the last remaining Le Mans camshaft, and really went to work on the engine. Apart from retaining the three-throw eccentrics camshaft drive, as against roller chain modification, the engine was brought up to the same specification as the Forrest Lycett power unit. When completed the bhp was 320 at 3,500 rpm. Incidentally, my car's wheelbase is 9 ft 6 in and its weight, wet, is 33½ cwt. At the same time the chassis was taken in hand, boxed full length, the brakes altered to hydraulic operation, a new instrument panel fitted, and the rear springs moved to outside the frame.

Panelcraft were responsible for a new and much lighter body and fuel tank. The latter weighed 20 lb and replaced a

In all its splendour—looking like a new car (or better) is Mr. Jupe's Speed-six after restoration. The owner stands alongside

40-gallon Le Mans type tank weighing 112 lb. From time to time small modifications like a new pressurised radiator and AC generator have been fitted.

Much-travelled Speed Six

We have always had a great regard for one of the rarer old Bentley models—the Speed Six. This car hit the headlines in a big way when it won at Le Mans in 1929 and 1930, and had the firm survived it would undoubtedly have been further developed for the big-car connoisseur. Basically, the car is a sporting version of the standard 6½-litre produced three or four years earlier. Its capacity is 6,597 cc and about 140 bhp

8

Economise . . . with a Bentley

R. J. Morpeth's account of life with an eleven-year-old Standard Steel Saloon recording 133,000 miles—without a rebore

I AM often asked why I use an older Bentley instead of purchasing a new popular saloon in the lower-capacity class. Thereby, it is suggested, I would safeguard myself against heavy outlay on maintenance and replacements besides having a more modern car; but would I save on annual depreciation? With my dateless, durable car I doubt it. Personally I have a preference for a solid roomy vehicle of good quality. Apart from that, however, I can find several other reasons in favour of a superlatively made good-class car a few years old, such as the Bentley Mark VI or R type. Too few motorists, I think, are prepared to buy an oldish car of this type although they may toy with the idea. Perhaps my own experience may help some of them to make up their minds.

My own car, illustrated here, was purchased, after looking over several, to take the place of a well-liked 3½-litre drophead Bentley that had given good service for several years. The "new" saloon, it will be seen, has the standard steel body and was new in 1951. With a known mileage of 119,000, twenty months ago it cost me £850. It is now showing 133,000 miles on the speedometer which, like all other instruments on the dashboard, has continued to work satisfactorily since purchase. Were I to sell the car now my monthly depreciation item would be decidedly moderate; but I intend to keep on running the Bentley.

There have been no major repair bills so far—only a few small items of inevitable expenditure on an old car. These include a new water pump, the short length of exhaust pipe between the two silencers, and the clutch facing on the mechanical servo renewed. All this has been done by a local firm for a total outlay of about £20.

I also fitted new Dunlops to the front wheels after I had covered 1,000 miles, and one maker's remould, Avon, at the rear. All the tyres seem good for at least another 10,000 miles and despite the weight of the car the remoulded cover has stood up satisfactorily. The front ones are showing no signs of patchy wear such as is often found with IFS. I do not change front tyres to back and *vice versa*, but careful attention is paid to correct inflation pressure. The Radiomobile radio has been trouble free.

The car is very comfortable for driver and passengers; the right-hand gear change is easy, light and positive, and the lever is so positioned that it causes no inconvenience when alighting from the driver's side of the car. It is sad to think that this most satisfactory mechanism is no longer offered by Bentley Motors (1931) Ltd., although users admit to occasionally being in third when top has been assumed to be in use, so silent is the box!

Interior condition is excellent with the original leather upholstery standing up well after eleven years use by three owners. Irvin seat harness has been fitted. The external condition of the car is obvious from the picture opposite

Like the gearbox the engine is quiet at all speeds up to the car's circumspect maximum of 85 m.p.h. It would probably still exceed that figure but I feel that it is high enough; and I do not overrev in the intermediates. Everything is still quiet at all speeds and no difficulty is experienced in hearing the radio when cruising in the upper seventies; wind noise with windows closed is negligible and not excessive at other times. The seating (hide) is in first-class condition, as one of the illustrations shows, and is very comfortable with its high backs and long, well-padded squabs. The interior trim of walnut is unmarked and looks well. The bodywork is free from rattles and perfectly watertight even in North Country downpours. Heating is better than with some more modern installations and does not overlook the rear seat passengers. I believe the arrangements on the current Bentley are particularly good. The demister, which has a separate motor, also works well. The screen washers function adequately and although the wipers are reliable they are a little slow in a heavy downpour; a modern two-speed replacement would be better. I have fitted Irvin harness for the front seats. It was very securely installed and is comfortable.

The car has a sunshine roof, an item not often found on recently manufactured British cars, although we pioneered the feature, I believe. The roof is still smooth-working and watertight. Undersealing was applied in the past, presumably by the makers, and the underside shows no signs of rust. The engine is fitted with a full-flow oil filter, which was not provided on earlier Crewe Bentleys. I believe this to be one of the reasons for the good condition of the engine, which has never been rebored. Earlier Mark VI cars, which had only the by-pass filter unit, do not seem to have been so long-wearing from what I have been told, although they have not been unsatisfactory by any standards. I always use Shell SAE 30—one grade heavier than recommended, but about right for a worn (presumably) engine.

As to running costs these are no heavier than those for the current 3-litre

BMC cars, with which I am also acquainted. To illustrate this point, I made a 300-mile run in the Bentley a short time ago and the same journey was later made in a fairly new, well-maintained Wolseley 6/99. The comparative petrol consumption for the trip was barely a couple of gallons more for the older, bigger-mileage Bentley, with the journey times practically the same. My usual petrol consumption when cruising in the 50-60 mph range is a good 20 mpg. If cruising in the 70-80 mph band it increases to 18 mpg, which I consider to be satisfactory. Bentleys are said to be oil consumers but I have not found the car unduly heavy; on a recent tour of 900 miles, three pints of oil were used.

Looking back over twenty pleasant motoring months, I would say that one of the best qualities the car possesses is its freedom from petty annoyances; irritating little things do not happen, nothing calls for early or frequent replacement. The car always maintains a full battery even on short runs in winter. I give the Exide (on the car) full marks, and also the Lucas "Special" electrical equipment. She starts well, even after standing for three or four winter hours in the open with side lights on; and I live on the North East Coast, not in Bournemouth!

The faithful old Bentley never seems to require small adjustments to carburetters, plugs or distributor points, although why this is so is hard to explain. Brakes require very infrequent adjustment. At a recent ten-year test the Churchill brake tester showed "excellent"; but then R-R drum brakes are famous.

I have only one point on which I am critical, and that is the steering. Although it is rather low geared, it is heavy when the car is being manoeuvred, which makes for hard work when parking in a narrow space. When moving even slowly, on the other hand, it is quite light—lighter in fact than some cars of much lower weight. Comfort is good, with the ride control a real asset on rough roads.

The accompanying illustrations give some idea of the present external and internal conditions of the car. Chromium plating is known to be very carefully done for these cars and this is reflected in its durability, which has been good. It may be noticed that I have done away with the original trafficators, and had flashers fitted; I have had fitted a pair of 1962 Volkswagen brake, tail and flasher units on the rear wings, and two yellow lights in the front of the car. This job, with wiring and making up faring for the rear lights, cost about £17 and is considered to be worthwhile alteration.

I have had two satisfactory experiences with Bentleys, the present one being a particularly good buy. Some motorists are chary of buying second-hand cars of any sort; and one with 119,000 miles on the clock would seem to them a "buying-trouble" purchase. There are, however, cars and cars and this Bentley has so far been one of the former! May it continue so for another 119,000 miles. Perhaps the present owner will put them on its clock.

Dated in appearance maybe, but the Mark VI still "has something". Bentley-supplied fitted trunks provide more luggage capacity than the boot size suggests

More Bentleys
The four-litre—an underrated car

The ohiv Cinderella model of the original firm is a better motorcar than most Bentley adherents and admirers claim, according to P. B. Balean who has known a particular Vanden Plas tourer since 1941 and owned it for three years

The curious and definable attraction of the Bentley marque which originated in the mind of one man of engineering genius, and existed for the short period of about ten years, is something I have always personally appreciated. The reputation of his designs has always been high—with one exception. I feel that the time has come to make a re-assessment of the 4-litre Bentley of 1930/31.

This model W. O. Bentley himself was never happy about, and considered that the engine, with its detachable Ricardo patented head, was rough and in a curious way responsible in some measure for the final failure of the company that he had largely built up.

I think one should at this stage mention that the L-shaped inlet-over-exhaust head, which Rolls-Royce acquired with the company in 1931, is in fact the basis of the present Rover engine, and the design was given by Rolls-Royce to Rover in exchange for certain secrets in connection with modern gas turbine engines for road use.

Of the four-litre Bentleys of 1930/31 only about fifty were produced and few remain. They used a shortened version the 8-litre chassis, and were either of about 11 ft 2 in 11 ft 8 in wheelbase. On this was usually placed a very hea saloon body, since the underlying idea of this model was compete with the comfort and silence of the 25 hp Ro Royce, and at the same time provide a better performan The bodymakers, however, rather impaired this scheme w their heavier saloons, but luckily Vanden Plas did buile limited number of fine open tourers, perhaps a dozen. So were four-door but the more handsome ones had only t doors. The weight of the complete saloon was perhaps 48 50 cwt, but the tourers probably scaled about 42 cwt.

When Bentley Motors went into liquidation and company was purchased by Rolls-Royce, three or four 3-li and 4½-litre vehicles were finished out of the parts that we taken over. Rumour has it that a few 4-litre saloons toure were also built out of remaining parts. This I think is untru

The cost of the 4-litre chassis was originally £1,225. complete vehicle therefore cost upwards of £1,500. Techni specifications are given at the end of this article.

In 1941 I was operational pilot in an Auxiliary Squadr and was fortunate enough to be allowed a generous petr ration for use on leave. My senior operational controller h purchased a Vanden Plas two-door 4-litre Bentley tour

and new in 1931, and this I was lent for leave motoring. ...ver the years the quality of this vehicle impressed me and ...ally I was able to acquire it in 1960. Since new it had very ...reful attention from one family chauffeur and was, as a ...sult, in quite astonishing condition. The total mileage, which ...had watched increase slowly for nearly twenty years, was ...en only something over 59,000 miles. The original owner, on ...nding the car over, remarked that he had had it much ...nger than most people nowadays kept their wives.

In spite of the affection with which it had been kept, and ...aintained, I felt that a thorough overhaul was deserved. The ...arbox and transmission were perfect, but a re-bore and the ...ting of oversized pistons—about 30 thou oversize—was ...und to be necessary. Oilways in the crankshaft were badly ...ocked by sludgy oil, and I now use a mildly detergent oil in ...ace of Castrol XXL as originally recommended and used for ...e entire life of the car.

The crankshaft was re-ground, quite a small amount, and ...l bearings refitted. Alan Smith of Derby, who is well known ...Reg Parnell's mechanical expert, then suggested that the ...ughness of which W. O. Bentley and Bentley enthusiasts ...mplained, might well be due to poor balance.

Accordingly, the crankshaft assembly, with flywheel and ...nnecting rods, were despatched to a particular firm at ...effield who specialise in that sort of thing. It was found that ...e crankshaft assembly and flywheel were 3 to 4 oz out on the ...wheel periphery and the connecting rods varied as much as ...oz in weight differential. These comparatively small ...easures in oz at thousands of rpm mean a very considerable ...lditional load on the crankshaft and bearings, and may be ...e of the reasons why Bentley enthusiasts have always ...garded the 4-litre Bentley as not only rough but also liable ...run No. 3 big end. The tappet block assemblies were

produce as a competitive rival model was in fact basically a successful venture. The Cricklewood company did, in fact, produce a model which could reasonably have competed with anything in the field at that time.

* * *

We might add a few comments to Squadron Leader Balean's interesting notes about the 4-litre Bentley. As we have understood the position, its evolution was a hasty and, events seemed to show, ill-advised attempt to produce a car that would appeal to a wider field than the existing Bentley following and potential. Both time and money were short at that critical stage and outside assistance (Ricardo & Co.) was used to evolve a reasonably-priced more "touring car" engine than the traditional Bentley ohc unit. This probably under-developed engine of quite new design was installed in a chassis, with a few alterations, that was originally used for the exceptional eight litre. We believe that Mr. Bentley had no part in the design of this "un-Bentleyish" engine. The 4-litre car without doubt hastened the end of the firm.

The author makes a categorical statement about Rolls-Royce and Rover in connection with the interchange of engineering knowledge or "secrets". This is most unlikely. Rover worked on the original Whittle gas turbine engine some time before Rolls-Royce took up this type of prime mover; and the ohiv combustion chamber in its modern form was not Crewe's exclusive property. In fact one of the leading engineers concerned with the Rolls-Royce/Bentley post-war car and industrial engines also had a very active share in the development of the Rover engine with the same basic type of valve arrangement.

As a matter of possible further interest, the writer of this postscript had a Swiss friend who bought a new 4-litre saloon and imported it into his country in 1931. He ran the car for

...fine vintage dashboard, with such interesting ...ems as a barometer and a column-type fuel guage. ...n opening windscreed was fitted, but the ...rcel shelf is non-standard

Twin SU carburettors are in evidence beneath the bonnet, as is the Autovac fuel feed and the adjustmeut on the steering box for column rake. The exhaust system on the offside has well arranged cast manifold, and the water pump is a true centrifugal unit

...faced at the overhaul, otherwise Alan Smith found very ...ttle additional work necessary before re-assembly.

There is absolutely no doubt in my own mind that the ...-balancing carried out has completely altered the running of ...e car. It is now smooth in operation and with 120 bhp ...puted to be under the bonnet is a really delightful car to ...rive. Brakes and cornering are well up to modern standards ...nd the bodywork has no irritating rattles, the doors close ...eautifully, the Tecalemit chassis lubrication system is a joy; ...nd the front bucket seats are vastly more comfortable than ...ost modern cars.

It is believed that the comparative performance figures for ...e 1931 4-litre Lancia Dilambda tourer and the Rolls-Royce ...0/25 tourer would show that what the Bentley firm set out to

many years to our knowledge and it satisfied his not very exacting demands. We rode in it on a number of occasions but never felt a desire to drive it. It was sluggish, rough-running and obviously a rather heavy handler: an un-distinguished representative of the marque in fact—apart from its impressive bonnet and radiator.

Had more money and time been available for further development the 4-litre Bentley might have been regarded in a much different light today by most Bentley enthusiasts. We have not previously heard that engine re-balancing can transform the general feel of the car; the author's view will interest many. The consensus of opinion is that the four-litre was an indifferent car because of its unpractical power to weight ratio. Taking a figure of 50 cwt (which we have heard

quoted on other occasions) and the power of 120 bhp mentioned by the author, we get a ratio of 48 bhp per ton. This was inadequate for a fairly expensive car of *circa* 1930/31; and it is astonishing to think that the board of Bentley Motors at that time thought such an underpowered car of such proud lineage had the slightest hope of commercial success.

In the light of these facts, it is a pity that when Squadron Leader Balean's engine was stripped and re-balanced, opportunity was not taken to ask Mr Alan Smith to raise the compression ratio, open out the ports, and generally apply his knowledge of power-increasing and tuning so as to raise the output to a safe 140/150 bhp. The car would then have been even more interesting. Perhaps this will be considered, and done—and another article prepared for us at a later date.—Ed.

SPECIFICATION of Four-litre Bentley
ENGINE:
26.8 hp, six cylinders, 85 by 115 mm (3,915 cc) 120 bhp at 4,000 rpm. Detachable head, overhead inlet valves, side exhaust valves, two carburettors, coil ignition. Compression ratio 5.5 to 1. Seven bearings. No vibration damper.

TRANSMISSION:
Dry single-plate clutch, separate four-speed gearbox with const mesh third. Ratios: 14.85, 7.81, 6.16, and 4.58 to 1; open prope shaft, spiral bevel final drive.

SUSPENSION:
Half-elliptic springs back and front, with friction front and hydra rear shock absorbers.

BRAKES:
Internal-expanding two-shoe brakes on four wheels, self-servo f brakes, direct mechanical operation.

MAIN DIMENSIONS:
Track 4 ft 8 in; wheelbase, 11 ft 2 in or 11 ft 8 in; overall w 4 ft 8½ in; length 15 ft 10¼ in or 16 ft 4¼ in; Ground clearance 7 turning circle right 47 ft, left 46 ft; tyres 20 x 6.5 in, pressure 3 per sq in; approximate chassis weight 32 cwt; author's Vanden tourer, 42 cwt; petrol tank capacity 20 gallons.

PERFORMANCE:
Speed in first gear, 25 mph; second, 40; third, 55/60; and top, Consumption 14-15 mpg; oil consumption 1,500 mpg. Comforta motorway cruising speed, 60/65 mph. Mileage when first seer 1941, 46,000; now 72,000.

Cockpit of the Blackham four-and-a half. The special control panel to the right of the wheel hinges to give access to the wiring a mounts a 15 amp master switch and switches for six lighting circuits, mogneto and coil ignition, SU fuel pumps, generator field, and test voltage. There is also a comprehensive system of warning lights

After the original Bentley Motors closed down, a handful of their cars was later assembled from new parts at the Rolls-Royce London service station. One of these is well-known to us and here is its interesting story.

In the above article the author refers to the well known fact that a number of "W.O." Bentleys were assembled at the London service station of Rolls-Royce Limited, after the old Bentley firm had failed and its assets purchased by the Derby company. A good deal of inaccuracy persists about this, however, the most common error concerning the time when this was done. The cars were *not* assembled almost immediately after the liquidation of the old firm but nearly five years afterwards. It has been stated with accuracy by the Bentley Drivers' Club just how many of these unusual cars were made, and which models. Six 4½-litre chassis were assembled and—a surprise to some enthusiasts—two three-litres.

Last month we dealt with a few interesting cars of Mr. W. O. Bentley's design and had space allowed we could have covered many more.

Last of the line
All these venerable cars—and many more for which we have not space—have a history, it will be noted, as well as a mechanical specification and performance of the greatest interest. No Bentley of the old type with which we have come into contact has a more intriguing life-story, however, than

Last of the line

the one owned by Mr. Philip Blackham, an engineer in publicity department of C.A.V. Limited, the Acton firm diesel engine fuel injection equipment specialists.

Mr. Blackham is the owner of one of the handful of W. type Bentleys that were built up from new parts by the Ro Royce-owned company as stated. These hybrid Bentle as we have heard them not really accurately called, have designation RC in front of their chassis number; we belie and we say this with some trepidation knowing the tremendo amount of Bentley knowledge existing among readers of motoring press, range from RC 41 to 46. The car owned Mr. Blackham is believed to be the first of those select f cars to be built up at the Bentley service station at Hend under the keen supervision of its manager, Mr. Clark. T particular car was built in 1936 and is RC41.

Mr. Blackham's car has a Vanden Plas body, although t might be questioned from an inspection of the pictures. The is no doubt about this, however, and the deviation from t classical line can be put down to a conservative moving w the times. For example, the wings are quite different to t traditional Vanden Plas long-flowing kind, and there a other subtle differences. A most interesting point about t body is that it is panelled in aluminium alloy and the wir are likewise of light metal.

This lighter 4½-litre has only had two owners, Mr. Blackha having had it in his possession for the past twelve years af keeping a watchful eye on the vehicle, interspersed by fruitle endeavours to negotiate a sale, for the previous five or years.

During his ownership Mr. Blackham has probably averag less than 3,000 miles a year of vintage motoring; at the mome the speedometer shows little more than 37,000 miles, b whether the total is 137,000 or approaching a quarter of million has not been established. The car has, however, be rebored once during its lifetime and now has lightened ov size Specialloid pistons. Originally the compression ratio v about 5.1 to 1 and then it was raised to just under 6 to 1. Af an exploratory period with this ratio the compression w brought up to its present figure of approximately 6.75 to

The flywheel has been lightened, the clutch slightly modified, but the camshaft and induction arrangements are standard. The most uncommon modification so far made is the conversion of the car to what in the old days was called dual-ignition; the offside magneto now functions merely as a contact breaker and distributor for coil ignition in order to ensure that there is a good fat starting spark at low cranking speeds. The nearside magneto is normal.

It will be remembered that the auxiliary drive arrangements of the bottom of the camshaft drive at the front end of Bentley four-cylinder engines comprises the cross-shaft for the two magnetos and another bevel drive for the water pump. This arrangement has on occasion been referred to as the Achilles heel of the design. Certainly the hardened steel bevels have given trouble on a number of older cars, doubtless due to advancing years allied to a much more lively engine than originally. To overcome this shortcoming some owners have fitted phosphor bronze gears but Mr. Blackham has discarded the mechanically-driven water pump and fitted a pump from a Rolls Royce 20/25. This is driven off the fanbelt pulley at the nose of the crankshaft; and as the pump is conveniently interchangeable with the standard unit no Heath-Robinsonian plumbing work spoils the classic appearance of the power unit. Moreover, it is an easy matter to remove the belt-driven pump at any time and replace it with the original, although this is not contemplated so satisfactory is the new arrangement. Another useful modification has been the fitting of a large and durable industrial diesel-engine silencer.

In the interests of good-looks, after a lot of contemplation the present owner of this unusual 4½ lowered the radiator about three-quarters of an inch and altered the bonnet hinges in order to get a slightly tapering bonnet line and, in his view, a rather better appearance than standard. For aesthetic reasons he has also lowered the windscreen about three-quarters of an inch and has narrowed the hood frame so that it fits inside the body and allows of a really neat and workmanlike furling of the hood.

In its present form the car turns the scale at about 36 cwt and it is believed that the engine puts out about 125 bhp. It is an ideal fast touring car for good British roads, handling in impeccable style; braking is good, if on the heavy side. The owner has therefore acquired a Clayton-Dewandre vacuum servo off a Speed Six Bentley. Discussions have taken place with Donald McKenzie regarding the fitting of this servo-motor but up to the time of writing this had not been done.

Everyone with interest but no great knowledge asks about the performance of these old cars. There seem to be two schools of thought. The first is the cynical, unbelieving who consider that all-out speed and accleration figures for these venerable cars compare with those of their own small-capacity family saloons. The highly enthusiastic, but equally badly informed, seem to have vague ideas that almost every vintage Bentley has the touch of McKenzie-Lycett magic about it. As usually, the truth is somewhere between these two extremes. In the case of Mr. Blackham's car, he has rather wisely never attempted to discover its maximum speed but it can comfortably cruise on the motorway at 75-80 mph. With the power and top gear ratio available, however, a maximum of fully 100 mph should be within this exceptional car's compass.

Mr. Phillip Blackham and his 1936 4½-litre Bentley, with Vanden Plas light-alloy coachwork reminiscent of that fitted to Lagonda cars of that period, as are the Lucas P100 headlamps and Windtone horns. The owner slighty lowered the radiator and bonnet, with a gain in appearance, and also modified the fold-flat screen in order to improve visibility

The B.7 BENTLEY with Automatic Transmission

The First Road Test of a British Car with Fully Automatic Gear-changing and Considerably Improved Performance

ONE does not expect a large percentage of potential purchasers of the Bentley class and price of car to be men of the Left willing to embrace any so-called reform merely because of its novelty. On the contrary one might reasonably suspect that a high proportion of Bentley buyers will tend conservatively to cling to the well known, and to well proved methods, and those of them who

NO OUTWARD SIGN reveals the changed mechanical character of the Bentley saloon in its automatic-transmission form; the classic body style lends itself particularly well to a two-colour finish, especially with the longer tail of the B.7.

LUGGAGE accommodation is greatly improved compared with earlier models, the spare wheel and tools still being separately housed, but leaving space for oddments at each side.

already have experience of the Bentley clutch and gearbox will have known the classic type of transmission in its finest manifestation. Of necessity, therefore, a road test of a Bentley fitted with the alternative automatic gearbox must first answer the questions: "In what fashion does this gearbox work?" "Does it change gear as well as a skilled driver?" "What effect has it on the acceleration, speed and fuel consumption of the car?"

When the driver takes his seat in the new model he finds that it is impossible to start the engine until the gear lever is placed in the neutral position. Once the engine is running the lever may conveniently be moved down a notch into the

position marked 4. There is no clutch pedal, and when the hand brake is released the car will move off, and using a bare minimum of throttle opening will pass through the three indirect gears with automatic changing so that there is direct drive by the time that 20 m.p.h. is attained. Should traffic demand a lower speed, or should the car be brought to rest changes down will automatically be made at about 15, 10 and 5 m.p.h.

One may immediately be critical in that such changes appear, on this class of car, to be unnecessary to be accompanied by a noticeable change in engine note, and by a slight shock as the additional engine braking is willy-nilly imposed on the car.

If we take a contrasting type of driving such as was used during our standing-start acceleration times, the accelerator is held wide open from rest up to maximum speed and in these circumstances the car will run up to approximately 20, 35 and 60 m.p.h. in the successive indirect ratios. It follows that by giving the car wide open throttle a change down will be made into third gear at any speed between 35 and 60 m.p.h.; and into second gear at any speed between 20 and 35 m.p.h.; and into bottom gear if the speed is below 20 m.p.h. These downward changes on full throttle are made smoothly, as well as silently, and the same may be said of all the upward changes of speed. Moreover, the box is itself almost noiseless.

Choice of Ratio

Having now described how the gears engage themselves in response to road speed and to the position of the accelerator, let us see what happens if the driver uses the steering column lever. By pulling this down from fourth to third position the third gear will be coupled up by means of an oil servo mechanism if the road speed is below 65 m.p.h. and above about 20 m.p.h. As there is no clutch the gear change is effected by moving the lever alone, and although this can cause some shock as the car is called upon to speed up the engine, a perfectly smooth change will be made if the throttle is opened up at the same time. In other words, the driver can use his skill both in the timing of a gear change and in performing the operation to the best possible advantage. These remarks apply in equal degree to the change down to second gear, which may be effected at speeds below 35 m.p.h.

HIGH-GRADE leather, finely polished wood and a general air of good taste characterize the Bentley's interior. Seen here are the deep front seats with sensibly shaped squabs.

Once the gear lever has been moved the gear selected remains engaged irrespective of throttle opening except for the fact that an automatic upward change will be made at peak speed; in other words, if one were to drive on full throttle downhill with the gear lever in second position an upward change would be made into third between 35 and 40 m.p.h., and from third to top at between 65 and 70 m.p.h. Automatic downward changes, ending in the coupling up of first gear are made below 15 m.p.h.

Enthusiasm Engendered

The enthusiastic driver will find this feature invaluable. The gears can be used normally to assist the brakes as when running down mountain passes; alternatively a long winding hill with a gradient of, say, 1 in 8 can be stormed up in the third gear which remains engaged even when the throttle is released when coming into a corner, there being perhaps one or two automatic changes between third and top if straight sections of the hill permit the speedometer to approach the 70 m.p.h. mark.

Some of the more enthusiastic may regret the elimination of the feeling of moral superiority engendered by the perfectly timed co-ordination of clutch and gear lever which is possible on the orthodox gearbox, but the possibility of keeping both hands on the steering wheel gives additional control over the car which is a valuable feature in high-speed cornering. To sum up, the new Bentley transmission gives perfectly smooth starts from rest, and quiet and smooth engagement of the gears either automatically or, with few exceptions as and when the driver wishes.

There must be many who think that multi-train epicyclic gearboxes involve additional friction losses which will be reflected in lower m.p.g. and reduced maximum speed, and others who are certain that no automatic gear-change can conceivably act so effectively as a skilled driver. Unless the testers on The Motor staff are less skilled than they think themselves to be, the acceleration times recorded by the Bentley immediately disprove the last-named belief.

The smooth start from full torque with the hydraulic coupling brings up 30 m.p.h. from rest in bottom gear as fast as it can be done with clutch slipping and wheelspin using the conventional transmission on the 1952 Mk. VI. By the time that second gear has been engaged, and 40 m.p.h. reached, the automatic changes shows to slight advantage, and after the change has been made from third to top gear at 70 m.p.h. the automatic transmission has saved 1.1/5 seconds. Even a standing ¼-mile proves to be better by 0.4 seconds.

This direct comparison is qualified by the fact that the final gear ratio on the Mark VI (3.73 : 1) was lower than the ratio used on the B.7 model, but the difference was not of a magnitude which should greatly affect the acceleration figures.

All Round Improvement

The idea that additional friction is present to impair fuel consumption is also disproved by the fact that a car with automatic transmission shows a 10% better consumption figure at 70 m.p.h. and better figures at all speeds down to 30 m.p.h. Finally, and here perhaps the change in final axle ratio played a more important part, the maximum speed of the car has been sensibly increased, the highest recorded speed in a favourable direction being little less than 105 m.p.h.

It is exceedingly rare for a well-established model to be modified, in the space of twelve months, so as to provide the buyer with higher speed, better acceleration, lower fuel cost and considerably increased ease in

driving. These substantial benefits do not, however, exhaust the dividends which have been declared by the Bentley engineering division.

The changes made to the rear of the frame and the body have not only increased very greatly the luggage-carrying capacity of the vehicle, but have also added a little over 1½ cwt. to the all-up weight and increased the unladen weight carried by the rear wheels from 2,000 to 2,235 lb. Coupled with some changes made to the rear spring location this has very much improved the high-speed handling of the car, and whereas on all the Mark VI models the degree of under-steer could be embarrassing, particularly on wet roads, with the B.7 a decisive but easily controlled breakaway at the back of the car can readily be induced. The driver thus finds himself far more "in command" than on previous types and in conjunction with the improved performance, and easier gear changing, appreciably improved average speeds over winding country roads are possible with increased safety.

In addition to the larger luggage boot the body for 1954 has a changed facia panel which provides superior reproduction from the inbuilt radio set, and a small tray which can be withdrawn from beneath the facia if needed.

It has been necessary to write so much in this report regarding the performance and handling of the car that little space remains to comment upon the host of general features which will commend it to owners looking for the ultimate in comfort and convenience. One may perhaps find excuse in the fact that in these respects the Bentley has already achieved an international reputation which is worthily maintained by the model which has recently been through our hands.

REAR-SEAT PASSENGERS enjoy the benefits of good legroom, comfortable arm- and foot-rests; built-in picnic tables pull out for use as shown here.

The **Motor** Road Test No. 9c/53 (Continental)

Make: Bentley   **Type**: B.7

Makers: Bentley Motors (1931) Ltd., 14-15 Conduit Street, W.1

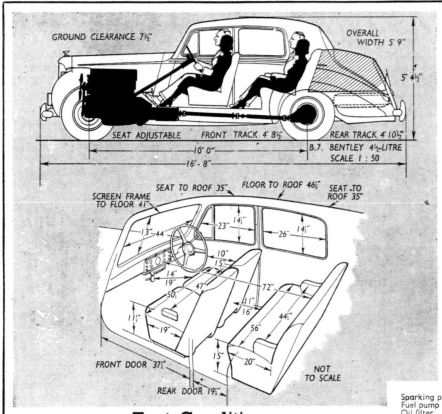

In Brief

Price £3170 plus purchase tax £1311 19s. 2d. equals £4481 19s. 2d.
Capacity ... 4,566 c.c.
Unladen kerb weight ... 38.1 cwt.
Fuel consumption ... 15.5 m.p.g.
Maximum speed 101.7 m.p.h.
Maximum speed on 1 in 20 gradient ... 91 m.p.h.
Maximum top gear gradient 1 in 9.2
Acceleration
10-30 m.p.h. 3 secs.
0-50 m.p.h. through gears 9.6 secs.
Gearing: 24.8 m.p.h. in top at 1,000 r.p.m.; 80.6 m.p.h. at 2,500 ft. per min. piston speed.

Specification

Engine
Cylinders	6
Bore	92 mm.
Stroke	114.3 mm.
Cubic capacity ...	4566 c.c.
Piston area ...	62.4 sq. in
Valves	Overhead inlet, side exhaust
Compression ratio ...	6.75/1
Carburetter ...	Twin S.U.
Ignition	coil
Sparking plugs	Champion N.8
Fuel pump	S.U. electrical
Oil filter	Full-flow

Transmission
Clutch ...	Hydraulic coupling
Top gear (S)	3.42
3rd gear (S)	4.93
2nd gear (S)	8.98
1st gear	12.93
Propeller shaft ...	Divided open
Final drive	Hypoid bevel

Chassis
Brakes	Hydraulic front, mechanical rear
Brake drum diameter ...	12¼ in.
Friction lining area...	186 sq. in.
Suspension:	
Front ...	Coil and wishbone I.F.S
Rear	Semi-elliptic
Shock absorbers:	
Front	Hydraulic
Rear	Hydraulic, with ride control
Tyres...	India, 6.50 x 16

Steering
Steering gear ...	Cam and roller
Turning circle	42 ft.
Turns of steering wheel, lock to lock ...	3¼

Performance factors (at laden weight as tested)
Piston area, sq. in. per ton ...	30
Brake lining area, sq. in. per ton...	89.4
Specific displacement	
litres per ton mile	2,730

Fully described in "The Motor," September 24, 1952, and October 14, 1953

Maintenance

Fuel tank: 18 gallon. Sump: 16 pints, S.A.E. 20 winter, 30 summer. Gearbox and differential 16 pints, Type A/AQ/ATS Castrol TQ, Donax T6 Mobiloil 3200. Rear Axle: 1¾ pints, Hipress S.C Steering gear: S.A.E. 30 Radiator: 30 pints (drain taps). Chassis lubrication: By pedal, one-shot system, S.A.E. 30. Ignition timing T.D.C. Spark, plug gap: 0.025 in. Contact breaker gap: 0.020 in. Valve timing Tappet clearances (cold): Inlet 0.006 in., exhaust 0.012 in. Front wheel toe-in: 0-1/16 in. Camber angle: 0 deg. Castor angle: ¼ deg. Tyre pressures: Front 25 lb., rear 30 lb. Brake fluid: Lockheed orange. Battery: 12 volt, 54 amp/hr. Lamp bulbs: Head lamps, 48 watt (Lucas pre-focus axial filament type 185) Side and tail lamps, 6 watt Centre lamp, 48 watt. Stop and reversing lamps, 6 watt

Test Conditions

Dry concrete road, warm weather, moderate diagonal wind. Premium-grade pump fuel.

Test Data

ACCELERATION TIMES (rolling start)

10-30 m.p.h.	3.00 sec.
20-40 m.p.h.	4.20 sec.
30-50 m.p.h.	5.50 sec.
40-60 m.p.h.	6.80 sec.
50-70 m.p.h.	9.10 sec.
60-80 m.p.h	12.35 sec.

MAXIMUM SPEEDS
Flying Quarter Mile

Mean of four opposite runs ...	101.7 m.p.h.
Best time equals	104.7 m.p.h.

Speed in Gears

Max. speed in 3rd gear	61 m.p.h.
Max. speed in 2nd gear	34 m.p.h.
Max. speed in 1st gear	21 m.p.h.

ACCELERATION TIMES from rest

0-30 m.p.h.	4.00 sec.
0-40 m.p.h.	6.65 sec.
0-50 m.p.h.	9.60 sec.
0-60 m.p.h.	13.25 sec.
0-70 m.p.h.	19.00 sec.
0-80 m.p.h.	25.10 sec.
Standing quarter mile	19.30 sec.

FUEL CONSUMPTION

21.8 m.p.g. at constant 30 m.p.h.
21.8 m.p.g. at constant 40 m.p.h.
19.8 m.p.g. at constant 50 m.p.h.
19.2 m.p.g. at constant 60 m.p.h.
16.5 m.p.g. at constant 70 m.p.h.
14.3 m.p.g. at constant 80 m.p.h.
Overall consumption for 569.4 miles, 36.7 gallons, equals 15.5 m.p.g.

WEIGHT

Unladen kerb weight	38.1 cwt.
Front/rear weight distribution...	48/52
Weight laden as tested	41.6 cwt.

INSTRUMENTS

Speedometer at 30 m.p.h. ...	accurate
Speedometer at 60 m.p.h. ...	5% fast
Speedometer at 80 m.p.h. ...	5% fast
Distance recorder	3% fast

HILL CLIMBING (at steady speeds)

Max. top gear speed on 1 in 20	91 m.p.h.
Max. top gear speed on 1 in 15	84 m.p.h.
Max. top gear speed on 1 in 10	69 m.p.h.
Max. gradient on top gear	1 in 9.2 (Tapley 245 lb/ton)
Max. gradient on 3rd gear	1 in 6.2 (Tapley 360 lb/ton)
Max. gradient on 2nd gear	1 in 4.3 (Tapley 521 lb/ton)

BRAKES at 30 m.p.h.

0.24g retardation (=125 ft. stopping distance) with 25 lb. pedal pressure.
0.52g retardation (= 58 ft. stopping distance) with 50 lb. pedal pressure.
0.73g retardation (= 41 ft. stopping distance) with 75 lb. pedal pressure.
0.83g retardation (= 36 ft. stopping distance) with 100 lb. pedal pressure.

Produced and built for the perfectionist— something near the ultimate in hand-made luxury— in fact, the

BENTLEY "S" SERIES

THERE is something extremely satisfying about sheer quality. One can be fascinated by the ingenuity of modern small car designers, who get a quart out of a pint pot. It is also entrancing to study mass production technique, as hundreds of identical saloons roll off the lines in a day. Yet, the hand-made quality car, built to a standard with mere cost an afterthought, probably exerts a greater attraction than ever it did.

I have had the good fortune to try most of the world's fine cars, but I have never seen anything to compare with the workmanship and finish of the new "S" Series Bentley. Particularly in the interior of the body, the absolute perfection of detail, and the excellent taste shown throughout, make almost any other car seem cheap and tawdry by comparison. This is a much bigger vehicle than any previous Bentley of the Rolls-Royce line. Among its ancestors, one must go back to the almost apocryphal 8-litre Bentley or the Phantom II Rolls-Royce for comparison. There is, in fact, a good deal to remind one of the "PII" about this car, though the similarity is difficult to put into words.

The design is entirely conventional, with helical springs and wishbones in front and a hypoid axle on semi-elliptic springs behind. Yet, there is much novelty in the detail work. The rear axle has a torque member above it which also acts as an anti-roll bar. It permits the use of long, supple springs without the embarrassments occasioned by "winding up" on acceleration, while functioning as a torsion bar against roll. It is displaced towards the offside of the axle to combat propeller shaft torque, and a two-way switch gives an electrical control to the rear dampers, the "hard" setting being useful when the body is heavily laden.

The box section frame, of great depth, has cruciform bracing, and the front suspension is reinforced by a normal anti-roll bar. The cam and roller steering box is coupled by a short, transverse link to the three-piece track rod with two slave arms. The propeller shaft is divided, and the usual Rolls-Royce centralized chassis lubrication system is fitted.

The engine is a remarkably big six-cylinder unit, of nearly 5-litres capacity. The exhaust valves are in the cast-iron cylinder block, and the push rod operated inlet valves are in the detachable head. The twin SU carburetters are of the new type with diaphragm seals, and there is an automatic cold-starting arrangement.

A fully automatic gearbox, with four forward speeds, is standardized. If de-sired, under exceptional conditions, the driver can override the mechanism and select a lower gear manually.

On taking one's seat, the Bentley feels a very big car. It has a long bonnet, but visibility is good. The engine starts by an extra movement of the ignition key, in line with current Continental and American practice. All the controls are as usual, except that the direction indicator is mounted on the facia instead of projecting from the steering column.

If the gear lever is placed in the normal driving position, a gentle pressure on the accelerator will cause the car to glide away. First and second speeds, being very low, are disposed of almost at once, but third is held for longer before the direct drive is engaged. Driven in this manner, the changes in and out of the two lower gears can be felt, but one seldom knows, or cares, whether third or top is being employed.

Violent use of the accelerator gives a very rapid getaway indeed. The big engine can then be felt and heard at work to some extent, till third speed is found, and all mechanical sensation virtually disappears. In comparison with the best American V8s, the six-cylinder Bentley engine is not quite so smooth in initial acceleration, but it has a gloriously long

DO NOT TOUCH: Not designed for owner-driver maintenance, the highly finished engine is not too accessible.

QUALITY of finish extends to the instrument and control layout, impeccably functional. There are now only two pedals.

ENTRANCE HALL: *The big car is luxuriously furnished, and dignity of entry and exit is assured. Note the folding tables.*

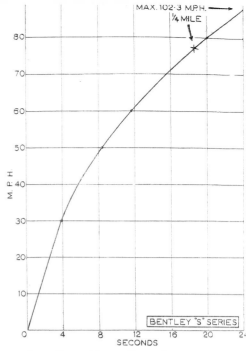

Acceleration Graph

stride which gives the most effortless high speed cruising imaginable.

The suspension is, if anything, on the firm side. The ride is very comfortable, and there are no sharp up and down movements, but there is not the slightest suspicion of transatlantic "float". I found that the softer position of the ride control gave the best roadholding, and I would only employ the harder setting if the large boot were full of luggage.

Very high marks indeed must be given to the new Bentley for its handling on wet roads. It is a fundamentally safe machine, and the method of locating the back axle has greatly improved the rear end behaviour compared with the previous model. Even on really greasy surfaces, there is a remarkable absence of wheelspin, because the springs are relieved of undesirable torque effects which would tend to promote axle patter or tramp.

As one covers the miles, there is a great sense of well-being. The seats, with their exceptionally high backs, may be set in a moment to any angle desired. The steering is not heavy, though no power assistance is provided. It is only when manœuvring or parking in a confined space that more work at the wheel is needed than in the case of a smaller car. A very elaborate heating and ventilating system is built in, so the windows may be kept closed under all normal conditions. The touch of a switch opens the flap over the petrol filler cap, so removal of the ignition key at once safeguards the fuel. There is a master key which will unlock the dashboard locker and the luggage boot as well as fitting the doors and ignition. An ordinary ignition key is also provided, with which the garage man can start the car, but he cannot gain access to your documents or baggage. The car is full of thoughtful ideas for the comfort and convenience of the occupants.

It is impossible to choose any "best" speed for the Bentley. Thus, there is no difference in mechanical sound if one cruises at 30 m.p.h. or 80 m.p.h. At the timed maximum speed of over 102

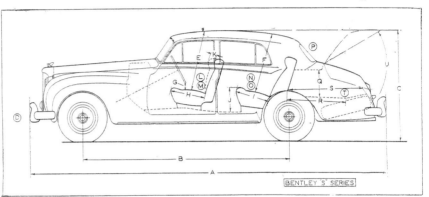

Dimensions

A Overall length, 17 ft. 7¼ ins.
B Wheelbase, 10 ft. 3 ins.
C Overall height, 5 ft. 4 ins.
D Overall width, 6 ft. 2¾ ins.
E Front head room, 3 ft. 1½ ins.
F Rear head room, 3 ft. 1 in.
G Steering wheel to seat cushion, 5 ins.
H Front seat depth, 1 ft. 7½ ins.
I Rear seat depth, 1 ft. 7 ins.
J Height of rear cushion, 1 ft. 3 ins.
K Front seat squab adjustment, 8 ins.
L Front seat width between arm rests, 4 ft. 1 in.

M Front seat width over arm rests, 4 ft. 5 ins.
N Rear seat width between arm rests, 3 ft. 9 ins.
O Rear seat width over arm rests, 4 ft. 6½ ins.
P Width of rear window, 3 ft. 10 ins.
Q Minimum depth of luggage compartment, 1 ft. 3½ ins.
R Length of floor of luggage compartment, 2 ft. 9 ins.
S Maximum length of luggage compartment, 3 ft. 10 ins.
T Overall width of luggage compartment, 5 ft. 5 ins.
U Door opening of luggage compartment, 6 ft. 2 ins.

m.p.h. the machine ran straight without conscious direction from the driver, and the engine still refrained from joining in the conversation. A speedometer reading of 110 m.p.h. was occasionally seen. Perhaps the most endearing characteristic of the car is its remarkable liveliness, in top gear, between 65 and 80 m.p.h. This facilitates overtaking, and is another potent safety feature.

For many years, Rolls Royce and Bentley models have rejoiced in a superb braking system. In spite of adopting the automatic system of transmission, the makers have been able to retain their traditional gearbox-driven servo motor. This controls the whole of the braking force on the front wheels and just over half the effort on the rear wheels, by hydraulic means. About 40 per cent. of the rear braking is still taken from a mechanical hook-up direct to the pedal. In this way, "feel" is retained, and two fully independent braking systems, either of which is complete in itself, are in operation at all times. As there are also tandem master cylinders, with two separate fluid bottles, there is still further duplication for safety.

This method of application really works, and the heavy car can be pulled up from high speeds with never a thought of brake fade. It is in this respect that the Bentley completely dominates American

The Bentley "S" – Specification and Performance

Car Tested: Bentley "S" Series 4-door sports saloon. Price £3,295 (£4,943 17s. with P.T.).

Engine: Six cylinders 95.25 mm. x 114.30 mm. (4,887 c.c.). Pushrod operated overhead inlet valves and side exhaust valves. Compression ratio 6.6 to 1. Twin SU carburetters. Lucas coil and distributor.

Transmission: Four-speed automatic gearbox, ratios 3.42, 4.96, 9.00 and 13.06 to 1. Open propeller shaft. Hypoid rear axle.

Chassis: Box section frame with cruciform bracing. Independent front suspension by wishbones and helical springs. Cam and roller steering box connected by transverse link to 3-piece track rod. Rear axle on semi-elliptic springs with combined torque resisting and anti-roll member. Piston-type dampers all round, with two-position electric control at rear. 8.20 x 15 ins. India tyres on five-stud disc wheels. Mechanical servo motor on gearbox operating front brakes entirely and rear brakes 60 per cent. hydraulically, in addition to

direct mechanical 40 per cent. application of rear shoes, in 11 ins. x 3 ins. cast iron ribbed drums.

Dimensions: Wheelbase, 10 ft. 3 ins. Track, front, 4 ft. 10 ins; rear. 5 ft. Overall length, 17 ft. 7½ ins.; width, 6 ft. 2½ ins. Height, 5 ft. 4 ins. Turning circle, 41 ft. 8 ins. Weight, 1 ton 19 cwt.

Equipment: 12-volt lighting and starting. Speedometer. Ammeter. Oil pressure, water temperature, petrol and sump level gauges with warning light. Two-speed self-parking wipers. Flashing direction indicators. Heater and demister. Radio. Clock. Spotlights, Picnic tables. Ladies' companions.

Performance: Maximum speed, 102.3 m.p.h. Speeds in gears (approx.), 3rd 67 m.p.h., 2nd 31 m.p.h. 1st 20 m.p.h. Standing quarter-mile, 18.8 secs. Acceleration: 0-30 m.p.h., 3.8 secs.; 0-50 m.p.h., 8.4 secs.; 0-60 m.p.h., 11.6 secs.; 0-80 m.p.h., 20 secs.

Fuel Consumption: Driven hard, 15 m.p.g.

cars of comparable size and speed. The brakes are just as powerful as those on last year's model, but a slight fierceness at very low speeds has now been completely eliminated.

The Bentley, "S" Series, is a very attractive big car with superb lines, appearance, and finish. It costs a lot of money, but to the connoisseur who must have the best, it is worth every penny of it. It is schemed to require the very minimum of attention over large mile-

ages, but it has the famed Rolls-Royce service behind it when any attention is required. A little on the large side in crowded city streets, it becomes a remarkably easy car to handle when the open country is reached. Only a few of us can aspire to own such a magic carpet, but to drive it is to advance another step in one's motoring education. This will still be a glorious car in 45 years' time, just as my own 1911 Rolls-Royce is to-day.

FINE PERFORMANCE: Ron Flockhart (Connaught) about to overtake Godia's Maserati in the Grand Prix of Europe at Monza. Connaughts took third and fifth places in this World Championship event.

The BENTLEY "S" Series

(with power steering)

DIGNIFIED and beautifully finished, the Bentley is a large and comfortably roomy car with well balanced lines.

Power Steering Added to a Top-class British 100 m.p.h. Car

BUILT with less regard for cost than almost any other car in the world, the Bentley "S" series saloon is very much in the British tradition of luxuriously furnished sports saloons. From the more ephemeral automobile designs of America, however, it has borrowed some of their more practical inspirations, the most recent being a hydraulic power-assisted steering system which, of British design and manufacture, has allowed the Bentley to match power-steered American cars in ease of parking.

Large and handsome enough for anyone to be proud to own it, the Bentley is a little less wide than some other big cars of today, and retains an impressively long bonnet as part of its 17 ft. 8 in. overall length. Fine proportions and uncramped overall length conceal from the eye the fact that, in an era of exaggeratedly low bodies, this car remains high enough built to be easy to enter and to offer ample interior headroom. So that it may be called a six-seater car, a bench type front seat has been fitted, but division of the backrest into two halves, each of which is individually adjustable for rake and carries a folding central armrest, restores most of the advantages which individual seats would otherwise offer.

No concessions have been made to transient fashions in the interior decoration of this car, which surrounds its owner with

traditional luxury. Inlaid woodwork is used for the facia panel and around the sides of the body, high quality leather is used to upholster really comfortable seats, and the carpeting is of soft pile. Interior equipment is comprehensive, front and rear passengers being separately provided with ashtrays, cigar lighters, picnic tables and other amenities.

Driving the Bentley or being driven in it, the first impression is of quiet, of a freedom from background noise utterly different from what is generally accepted as "silence" in more popular types of car. Not only are sounds produced by the Bentley's own movement virtually absent, both noise from the engine and the rumble of wheels rolling on the road, but there is also a high degree of insulation from the noise and turmoil of the outside world such as a really well-built house can provide. Starting up the car from cold, the automatic choke inconspicuously yet effectively looks after the engine's warming-up period, and with the automatic gear selector moved to its usual "4" position (to allow any of the four gears to engage as required) the car moves smoothly through traffic in response to a light touch on the accelerator pedal.

A light touch on the controls suffices for all driving of this car, which apart from the automatic transmission also has hydraulic power assisted steering and mechanical power assisted brakes. Maximum retardation is provided for a brake pedal pressure of only 50 lb., no more than half the pedal effort often regarded as perfectly acceptable on much smaller cars. High performance and heavy build can load a braking system severely, a single rapid stop from around the Bentley's top speed ending in an aroma of hot lining material, but there is good resistance to fade and excellent smoothness in hard braking. Around town, a driver

must be careful if he is not to jerk the car, because a delay of a few inches of car movement before the gearbox-driven servo takes effect makes it near-instinctive to press unnecessarily hard on the brake pedal when crawling in stop-go traffic.

In applying hydraulic power assistance to the steering, the Bentley designers have arranged for the pressure from an engine-driven pump to take effect only when a force greater than approximately 2 lb. is applied to turn the steering wheel to left or right. Thus, in straight-road driving, almost normal "feel" of rather low-geared steering with a modest amount of self-centring action is retained. In low-speed manoeuvres or in fast cornering, however, resistance to steering wheel movement does not build up further in the manner that would be expected without the servo. Especially welcome to buyers who do a lot of town motoring, the optional power steering is less of an asset for fast driving, being no quicker in response than ordinary steering if a skid on a slippery road must be checked, but needing to be known before fast double swerves can be tackled with really confident precision because there is no longer strict proportionality between the force applied to the steering wheel rim and that generated between tyres and road. Power assistance does not seem to have robbed the steering mechanism of the especial mechanical smoothness and precision long associated with the controls of cars built in the Rolls-Royce factory.

Our test of this Bentley took place during a period of unbroken fine weather, but apart from extreme sensitivity to cross-winds during fast driving we found the roadworthiness of this latest chassis highly commendable. Riding comfort was also good, especially for the rear seat passenger who was far more completely insulated from road shocks than the conventional

In Brief

Price (including power-assisted steering as tested): £3,605 plus purchase tax £1,803 17s. 0d., equals £5,408 17s. 0d.
Price without power steering (including purchase tax), £5,243 17s. 0d.

Capacity		4,887 c.c.
Unladen kerb weight ...		39¼ cwt.
Acceleration:		
20-40 m.p.h. in kick-down gear		4.2 sec.
0-50 m.p.h. through gears		9.2 sec.
Maximum direct top gear gradient		1 in 8.1
Maximum speed ...	...103.6 m.p.h.
"Maximile" speed ...	...100.8 m.p.h.
Touring fuel consumption ...	16.1 m.p.g.

Gearing: 24.8 m.p.h. in top gear at 1,000 r.p.m.; 33.1 m.p.h. at 1,000 ft./min. piston speed.

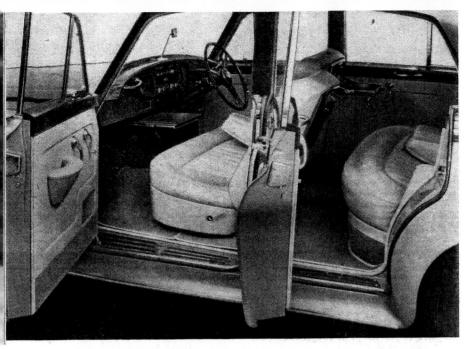

AMENITIES provided inside the four-door body include removable side armrests, folding central armrests, adjustable-rake backs to the front seat, folding picnic tables, and a heating system with a direct supply of warmed air to the rear compartment.

use of semi-elliptic springs and a rigid axle might lead anyone to expect. Use of a two-position switch on the steering column to set the rear shock absorbers to "hard" for fast open road driving checks a slight "floating" action, and restoring the switch to "Normal" minimizes shake over cobbled town streets. Fast cornering does not produce much body roll, but the tyres do squeal rather loudly if a driver handles this luxury saloon in the manner more appropriate to a sports car.

As the figures on the data page show, the maximum speed of the Bentley is now well over 100 m.p.h., a timed speed of 105 m.p.h. being exceeded with a slightly favourable wind. Nowadays the automatic gearbox, built and refined in Britain on the basis of the best-tried American design, is generally very smooth, and a rest-to-90 m.p.h. acceleration time of less than 35 seconds indicates that it provides plenty of performance. There remains an unhappily wide gap between 2nd and 3rd ratios, but the acceleration in 3rd gear from 35 m.p.h. onwards is rapid enough to make this gap much more forgivable than it was on earlier models.

Although the transmission is fully automatic, with a fluid flywheel replacing the old-style clutch and with changes of ratio in the epicyclic 4-speed gearbox taking place in accordance with speed and throttle opening, ample over-riding control is now provided for the driver. At speeds above about 30 m.p.h., the automatic transmission

will not automatically change out of top gear when the car is accelerated unless a definite "kick-down" second pressure is applied to the accelerator pedal, so that all the smooth and silent but very powerful torque of the 4.9-litre engine can be used for effortlessly brisk top-gear acceleration. By moving the gear selector from "4" to "3" however, a driver can effect a smooth change down from top to 3rd gear in advance of needing full acceleration to overtake another vehicle, or he can save his brakes by selecting either 3rd or the very

low 2nd gear in appropriate circumstances. Location of the gear selector lever in a stepped quadrant means that the lever can be moved between the "4" and "3" settings or between the "3" and "2" settings entirely by feel, without any need to look down at the controls, it being further necessary to press a button on the tip of the selector lever before neutral or reverse gear can be selected.

If the windows are kept closed, the Bentley remains an extremely quiet car right up to its maximum speed, and is very restful for fast cruising along a modern motor road. It is unfortunate that, whilst a complete refrigeration system of some complexity is available for tropical climates, the ordinary heating and ventilation system delivers only rather limited volumes of fresh air into the car, so that frequently it seems desirable to open a window and thereby sacrifice silence. The controls for this system work with delightful ease, and it is possible to have cold de-misting air directed on to the windscreen even when the heater is in use. but three-position "off-cold-hot" air temperature controls make less concession to varying personal climatic tastes than is appropriate to a 1957 luxury car. Run at half speed, the separate heater and de-mister fans are inaudible even in this very quiet car, and at the full speed setting they are still far from noisy. Commendably, some air from the heater is ducted directly to the floor of the rear compartment, and electrical heating is provided to de-mist or de-frost the rear window in winter.

CARPETED and with the spare wheel separately accommodated, the luggage compartment is of quite large area and is internally lit after dark. Opening of the fuel filler cover is either electrically from the facia panel or manually from inside the boot.

SWEPT lines characterize the rear view, details of which include reversing lamps and an anti-mist heated rear window of ample size.

are not normally visible include a one-shot chassis lubrication system operated by a pedal below the facia panel (one "shot" every 200 miles is suggested), and use of a twin contact-breaker type of ignition distributor on the six-cylinder engine.

Impressively good-looking and exceptionally comfortable, fast but with a new-found ease of handling in congested cities, the Bentley "S" series is a dual-purpose car. Delightful when judged from the rear seat with a skilled chauffeur at the wheel, it is also a car which an owner or his wife could enjoy driving personally, and whilst its interior furnishing is of a kind which asks to be treated with more respect than is

Very much to our taste are the Bentley instruments, quite comprehensive, and with a sensible black speedometer dial of circular shape on which all readings were almost precisely honest. Also most pleasing was a twist-to-release pull-out handbrake, of the general type which is familiar in America but built to Rolls-Royce standards of smooth efficiency. Also very comfortable to handle is the familiar rigid-spoked steering wheel, with a consistently responsive horn button at its centre, there being no engine vibration to make spring spokes in the steering wheel necessary for comfort. The full lighting system includes

FINE grained woodwork, and a full set of instruments with clear white figuring on black dials, form the facia panel. Control over the automatic gearbox may be exercised by a keen driver, using a small lever which moves in a stepped quadrant behind the steering wheel.

two foglamps and a reversing lamp, but of headlamp effectiveness we cannot speak as yellow bulbs of utterly unsuitable type had been fitted in anticipation of Continental motoring. Mechanical refinements which

sometimes accorded to the painted interior metalwork and washable plastic roof linings of more popular-priced cars, this model is very evidently built to provide many miles and years of good motoring.

Specification

Engine

Cylinders ...	...	...	...	6
Bore	...	...	...	95.25 mm.
Stroke	...	...	...	114.3 mm.
Cubic capacity	...	...	...	4,887 c.c.
Piston area	...	...	...	66.25 sq. in.
Valves	...	...	...	Overhead inlet

(pushrod operated), side exhaust

Compression ratio ...	...	6.6/1
Carburetter	...	2 S.U. type H.D.6

(diaphragm type)

Fuel pump...	...	S.U. dual electric, type L
Ignition timing control	...	Centrifugal
Oil filter	...	British Filters, full flow
Max. power	... ...	—

Transmission

Clutch	...	Fluid coupling and automatic gearbox
Top gear ...	... ...	3.42
3rd gear ...	... ...	4.96
2nd gear ...	... ...	9.00
1st gear ...	... ...	13.06
Reverse ...	... ...	14.72
Propeller shaft	Hardy Spicer divided open
Final drive	...	12/41 hypoid bevel
Top gear m.p.h. at 1,000 r.p.m.		24.8
Top gear m.p.h. at 1,000 ft./min. piston speed ...	...	33.1

Chassis

Brakes	...	Hydro-mechanical with gearbox-driven mechanical Servo
Brake drum internal diameter...		11¼ in.
Friction lining area	...	240 sq. in.

Suspension:

Front ... Independent by coil springs, wishbones and anti-roll torsion bar

Rear ... Semi-elliptic springs, rigid axle, and "Z bar" torque reaction member

Shock absorbers ... Rolls-Royce double-acting piston type hydraulic (adjustable at rear).

Steering gear ... Cam and roller (power assistance optional extra)

Tyres ... ... 8.20—15 tubeless

Coachwork and Equipment

Starting handle	None
Battery mounting	Below luggage locker floor
Jack	Smiths Bevelift pillar type
Jacking points ...	External, below central body pillars

Standard tool kit: Jack, wheelbrace, wheel disc remover and tommy bar, tyre pressure gauge, tyre pump, feeler gauge, screwdriver, drain plug key, pliers, adjustable spanner, combination spanner, distributor spanner, sparking plug spanner, tappet spanner, 2 d/e ring spanners, spare bulbs, sachet of coolant corrosion inhibitor.

Exterior lights: 2 Lucas R700 headlamps, 2 foglamps/flashers, 2 sidelamps, 2 stop/tail lamps, number plate/reversing lamp.

Number of electrical fuses ...	9
Direction indicators ...	Flashers (amber) self-cancelling
Windscreen wipers ...	Two-speed two-blade electrical, self-parking
Windscreen washers	Trico, vacuum-operated
Sun vizors	Two

Instruments: Speedometer with decimal trip distance recorder, clock, oil and fuel contents gauge, oil pressure gauge, coolant thermometer, ammeter.

Warning lights: Low fuel level, direction indicators, headlamp main beam.

Locks:

With ignition key: Ignition switch, either front door.

With master key: Ignition switch, either front door, glove box, luggage locker.

Glove lockers	One on each side of facia panel
Map pockets ...	One in each front door
Parcel shelves ...	Behind rear seat
Ashtrays	One on facia panel, two behind front seats
Cigar lighters ...	One front, two rear

Interior lights: Roof light, 2 rear quarter lights, map reading light.

Interior heater: Fresh air type; heater (front and rear compartments) and de-misters have separate air volume and temperature controls.

Car radio ... ... Radiomobile 200X (7-valve), fitted as standard

Extras available: Power assisted steering, tropical air refrigeration equipment.

Upholstery material ...	English hide
Floor covering ...	Pile carpet

Exterior colours standardized: 4 two-tone combinations and 8 single colours (any special colour available at extra cost).

Alternative body styles ... Coachbuilt bodies by leading makers, to order

Maintenance

Sump ... ... 16 pints S.A.E. 20 for temperate summer and winter

Gearbox and fluid coupling: 2 pints, automatic transmission fluid type "A," spec. AQ/ATF.

Rear axle 1½ pints S.A.E. 90 hypoid gear oil

Steering gear lubricant: Power steering, automatic transmission fluid AQ/ATF; manual steering, S.A.E. 30 oil.

Cooling system capacity 28 pints (2 drain taps)

Chassis lubrication: By grease gun every 10,000 miles to 3 points, other points supplied with oil from pedal-operated pump.

Ignition timing ...	2° b.t.d.c.
Contact-breaker gap ...	0.019-0.021 in.
Sparking plug type...	Lodge CLNP or Champion N8BR
Sparking plug gap ...	0.025 in.

Valve timing: Inlet opens at t.d.c. with 0.030 in. tappet clearance.

Tappet clearances (cold):

Inlet ...	...	...	0.006 in.
Exhaust ...	...	...	0.012 in.
Front wheel toe-in ...	...	...	1/16 in.-⅛ in.
Camber angle ...	...	...	Zero

Castor angle: 0°-½° positive with power steering, ¼°-1° negative with manual steering.

Steering swivel pin inclination 4½° at zero camber

Tyre pressures (normal touring use, power assisted steering):

Front ...	...	...	21 lb.
Rear ...	...	...	26 lb.

Brake fluid ... Wakefield-Girling crimson

Battery type and capacity: Dagenite 6.HZP.9/GZ or Exide 6.XCV-9L, 57 amp. hr. at 20 hr. rate (negative earth).

The **Motor** Road Test No. 27/57 (Continental)

Make: Bentley   **Type:** "S" Series (with power steering)

Makers: Bentley Motors (1931) Ltd., 14-15 Conduit Street, W.1

Test Data:

World copyright reserved; no unauthorized reproduction in whole or in part.

Conditions: *Weather: Warm and dry with strong diagonal wind. (Temperature 47°-64° F., barometer 30.1-30.2 in. H.) Surface: Smooth concrete (Ostend-Brussels motor road). Fuel: Premium-grade pump petrol, approx. 95 Research Method Octane Rating.*

INSTRUMENTS
Speedometer at 30 m.p.h.   3% fast
Speedometer at 60 m.p.h.   accurate
Speedometer at 90 m.p.h.   accurate
Distance recorder   ...   1½% slow

WEIGHT
Kerb weight (unladen, but with oil, coolant and fuel for approx. 50 miles)   39¼ cwt.
Front/rear distribution of kerb weight   ...   49/51
Weight laden as tested ...   43¼ cwt.

MAXIMUM SPEEDS
Flying Half Mile
Mean of four opposite runs   ...   103.6 m.p.h.
Best one-way time equals   ...   105.3 m.p.h.

"Maximile" Speed (Timed quarter mile after one mile accelerating from rest.)
Mean of four opposite runs   ...   100.8 m.p.h.
Best one-way time equals   ...   102.3 m.p.h.

Speed in Gears (automatic change-up speeds at full throttle)
Max. speed in 3rd gear ...   ...   67 m.p.h.
Max. speed in 2nd gear   ...   36 m.p.h.
Max. speed in 1st gear ...   ...   23 m.p.h.

FUEL CONSUMPTION
23.5 m.p.g. at constant 30 m.p.h. on level.
21 m.p.g. at constant 40 m.p.h. on level.
19 m.p.g. at constant 50 m.p.h. on level.
18 m.p.g. at constant 60 m.p.h. on level.
16.5 m.p.g. at constant 70 m.p.h. on level.
14 m.p.g. at constant 80 m.p.h. on level.
11.5 m.p.g. at constant 90 m.p.h. on level.

Overall Fuel Consumption for 682 miles, 45.5 gallons, equals 15.0 m.p.g.(18.9 litres/100 km.)

Touring Fuel Consumption (m.p.g. at steady speed midway between 30 m.p.h. and maximum, less 5% allowance for acceleration). 16.1 m.p.g.

Fuel Tank Capacity (maker's figure), 18 gallons

HILL CLIMBING at sustained steady speeds
Max. gradient on top gear: 1 in 8.1 (Tapley 275 lb./ton).
Max. gradient on 3rd gear: 1 in 5.8 (Tapley 380 lb./ton).
Max. gradient on 2nd gear: 1 in 3.5 (Tapley 620 lb./ton).

STEERING
Turning circle between kerbs: left, 39¾ ft.; right, 39½ ft.
Turns of steering wheel from lock to lock, 4¼.

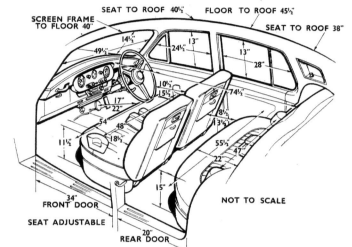

TRACK:— FRONT 4'-10" REAR 5'-0"
OVERALL WIDTH 6'-2¼"
23¼"   11¼"   GROUND CLEARANCE 7"
5'-4"   22¼"   10½"
SCALE 1:50   10'-3"   BENTLEY "S"
17'-8"

SCREEN FRAME TO FLOOR 40"   SEAT TO ROOF 40½"   FLOOR TO ROOF 45½"   SEAT TO ROOF 38"
14½"   49½"   24½"   13"   13"   28"   10½"   15½"   17"   22"   7¼"   8½"   13¼"   54"   48"   18½"   11¼"   55½"   47"   22"   34" FRONT DOOR   15"   NOT TO SCALE
SEAT ADJUSTABLE   20" REAR DOOR

ACCELERATION TIMES from Standstill			
0-30 m.p.h.	...	...	3.9 sec.
0-40 m.p.h.	...	...	6.5 sec.
0-50 m.p.h.	...	...	9.2 sec.
0-60 m.p.h.	...	...	13.1 sec.
0-70 m.p.h.	...	...	17.9 sec.
0-80 m.p.h.	...	...	24.7 sec.
0-90 m.p.h.	...	...	34.9 sec.
Standing quarter mile	...		18.9 sec.

ACCELERATION TIMES from rolling start			Direct top gear	Kick-down condition
0-20 m.p.h. ...	...	...	—	2.3 sec.
10-30 m.p.h. ...	...	...	—	2.8 sec.
20-40 m.p.h. ...	...	...	—	4.2 sec.
30-50 m.p.h. ...	...	...	8.3 sec.	5.3 sec.
40-60 m.p.h. ...	...	...	8.8 sec.	6.6 sec.
50-70 m.p.h. ...	...	...	10.5 sec.	8.7 sec.
60-80 m.p.h. ...	...	...	12.4 sec.	11.6 sec.
70-90 m.p.h. ...	...	...	17.0 sec.	17.0 sec.

BRAKES from 30 m.p.h.
0.84g retardation (equivalent to 36 ft. stopping distance) with 50 lb. pedal pressure.
0.55g retardation (equivalent to 54½ ft. stopping distance) with 25 lb. pedal pressure.

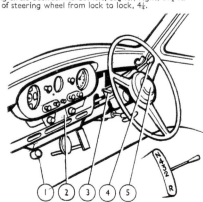

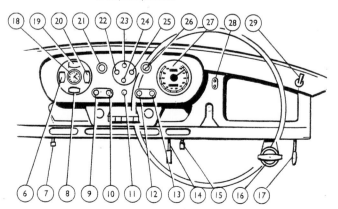

1, Headlamp dip switch. 2, Radio. 3, Ride control (down normal, up hard). 4, Gear selector. 5, Horn. 6, Coolant thermometer. 7, Clock regulator. 8, Amp meter. 9, Demister. 10, Wipers. 11, Oil level indicator button. 12, Instrument light and map light. 13, Heating. 14, Chassis lubrication pump. 15, Trip regulator. 16, Hand brake. 17, Bonnet catch (offside). 18, Clock. 19, Fuel gauge. 20, Oil gauge. 21, Cigar lighter. 22, Ignition warning light. 23, Light switch. 24, Ignition and master key switch. 25, Fuel warning light. 26, Petrol filler cap release. 27, Speedometer with mileage. 28, Charging plug. 29, Trafficator control.

The 4½-litre Bentley Continental Saloon

A Quiet and Comfortable Car Which Cruises at 100 m.p.h.

THE 4½-litre Bentley Continental saloon is one of the most expensive cars in the world and it is impossible to ignore this factor when assessing its qualities by means of a road test.

The team who take over such a car in order to pass judgment must first condition their own attitude so that it falls into line as nearly as possible with that of a potential owner to whom a considerable outlay on personal transport represents normal practice, and moreover one to whom the ownership of other types of motorcar for specific purposes may well be customary.

The Continental provides an alternative to those who require something even more spectacular and attractive in performance than that provided by the normal Bentley saloon which was introduced soon after the war and which has achieved a considerable reputation as well as surprisingly large sales for so high a quality (and therefore expensive) machine. The demand for an even faster and lower version was, however, soon heard, particularly from America, and following upon the introduction of the Continental last year the output was at first devoted to the export market. Now the car is available to order either at home or abroad and the version which we tested represents the original specification. Such minor modifications as have since taken place are set out in the caption to a photograph appearing in this test, but they make no difference to the handling or the performance of the car, and it may be assumed that the version which we tried was in fact very representative of the marque.

At first sight the light-weight Mulliner body and lowered radiator combine to provide a distinguished but by no means remarkable appearance. On subsequent contemplation, however, the thoroughbred lines of the car become increasingly attractive and it is notable that when the Bentley is taken into foreign countries where passers-by pay particular attention to such matters, the appreciative remarks come thick and fast, and a roadside halt quickly produces a respectfully admiring audience.

Four-country Test

It did not seem reasonable to assess the Bentley without a high-speed tour of Europe and for this purpose the car was driven first to Le Mans and thence to Belgium for the performance test. Thereafter a sortie to the Nurburgring in Germany provided the final and perhaps most valuable test evidence of fast mountain driving so that a true cross section of conditions were encountered in a matter of a very few days.

The journey to Central France was made by a crew of four and although no doubt one more could be crowded into the car in emergencies, comfort suggests that a driver and three passengers should be the limit for a long run. As to luggage space, the sloping tail and neatly-covered spare wheel with tools recessed into the floor gives surprisingly adequate room if the suitcases happen to conform to the best advantage. Anyone owning the car would do well to have a fitted set of luggage if four persons' kit is to be carried

As to the seating space and general comfort, this is of a very high order and forward visibility from the driver's point of view is excellent. While dealing with passenger comfort the important question of suspension must be discussed. For all normal purposes the ride control which

INTERIOR woodwork is in polished walnut, the facia carrying dials with clear white instruments on black faces. On the left can be seen the heater unit, and adjacent to it the one-shot lubrication pedal. Front seats are separate, with the usual Bentley gear lever on the floor at the right. The rear seat has a folding armrest, beneath which may be seen the fresh-air duct, near the floor.

so flexible is the high gear performance that the Bentley may claim a dual personality adaptable to entirely different mood and method.

Tribute must be paid to the brakes. Aided by the well-known Bentley servo mechanism the car retains its almost unique stopping power over the full range of speed and throughout the most trying circumstances that it is possible to devise.

The 4½-litre Bentley Continental Saloon - Contd.

governs the activity of the rear shock-absorbers can be left at its minimum setting.

On the car tested the fresh air supply, which could be obtained by opening a sliding panel, directed a great deal of air upon the driver's right ankle, but on later models this has been more evenly distributed. Also, on the car concerned, the heater fan was excessively noisy and somewhat naturally it was impossible to use the windows and louvres for ventilation purposes without considerable wind roar at high speeds. With everything closed the Bentley retains its very high degree of silence right up to maximum speed and the only audible indication that considerably more h.p. is available than on the standard version is a pronounced snarl from the exhaust pipe if the engine revolutions are caused to rise somewhat suddenly.

Matter of Choice

Minor matters of comfort and convenience on a car of this type are virtually decided by the prospective owner. Many variations on the theme can obviously be obtained and inspection of the four different Continental Bentleys to be seen in and around Le Mans during the race period revealed a considerable diversity of equipment.

To justify itself the Continental Bentley must handle superbly and offer a degree of continuous performance not readily obtainable elsewhere. The car, therefore, was driven at all times exceedingly hard and no great concession was ever made to gradient or surface. The steering has that slight reaction to road shocks which is a feature of many fine and fast motorcars. The accuracy with which this comparatively big machine can be placed and its total disregard for camber combine to make high average cruising an effortless affair. How rapid this cruising speed may be was demonstrated by a 20-mile journey over a fine motor road run in the normal course of business at an average of just

THE FLOWING tail contains a long, wedge-shaped luggage locker, in which the spare wheel is carried within a protective cover. Tools are housed separately beneath the boot. Twin reversing lamps are fitted. The photograph above shows how the large quarter-lights can be hinged open as air extractors.

over 80 m.p.h., and this despite reasonably heavy traffic and a natural desire not to inconvenience other road users.

It must, however, be recorded that on a subsequent occasion on wet concrete the Bentley felt somewhat unhappy at speeds in excess of 80 m.p.h. The tyres on the car at the time of this occurrence were worn fairly smooth and a light wind was blowing across the route. Under such conditions there is a need for considerable delicacy of touch from the driver if fast averages are to be achieved in the rain.

It will be seen that the gear ratios are remarkably close, and if full use is made of this fact acceleration is very rapid. In the normal course of touring the car is taken up to 50 on second, and perhaps a little more than 85 in third. Thence the needle climbs rapidly and the driver soon discovers the surprising and wholly delightful experience of throttling back to a cruising speed of a little over 100 m.p.h., at which figure the car sails along with consummate ease and silence.

Full use of the gearbox is by no means obligatory and the car will accelerate away very briskly in top gear from 10 m.p.h. without snatch or other protest. Indeed,

On the spectacular Nurburgring, several miles of the hardest imaginable work did certainly produce an exceedingly warm smell but there was no serious degree of fade or any need to increase appreciably the pressure applied to the pedal.

Driving the car in the Eiffel mountains showed how well the compromise between racing performance and touring comfort has been achieved. It also revealed the apparent indestructibility of the whole mechanism and the impression was gained that only barbarous driving methods or lack of elementary service could blunt the edge of this superb machine. On the question of maintenance the chassis lubrication system, which is operated from a pedal in the cockpit, enables the long-distance foreign tour to be accomplished without delays in the greasing bay.

There are, of course, minor criticisms. Although the owner is more likely to open the bonnet to display the splendour of the engine than to have to do anything to it, it is in either case annoying that only one side can be raised at a time. Headlights carried the yellow-type bulb which is now compulsory in France, and that may have been the reason that the illumination was poor. The fact remains that nothing like the full touring speed of the Bentley could be used at night. Conversely, although the horn sounded positively bashful to the occupants its penetration power on several occasions proved surprisingly adequate.

To sum up, the Continental Bentley undoubtedly takes its place as one of the world's great automobiles. Its most valuable features are the least noticed in a short journey. It is only after living with the car for days and nights of high-speed European travel that the true merit of this remarkable machine begins to make itself apparent.

CURRENT MODELS of the Continental differ from the car tested in that they have a slightly revised wing line, a one-piece windscreen and a dummy radiator cap with Bentley motif, as seen here.

FAST and SLINKY—ITS

Town carriage or open high-performance car the 4.9 litre Bentley Continental by Park Ward is clean and graceful. Aerodynamic efficiency is high in spite of an "old-fashioned" radiator. Chromium decoration is restrained and the elegant appearance is produced by body panels of delicate curvature

From the rear the Continental still maintains its dignified, luxurious appearance and blends well with this woodland setting. The rear bodywork is protected from knocks by really substantial bumpers with solid overriders. Beautifully-shaped rear wings have shallow fins and neat rear light clusters

SPORTS CARS ILLUSTRATED

EVEN in this atomic age, 120 m.p.h.-plus machines are by no means commonplace. Perhaps this is just as well judging by the antics of some of our less skilled week-end drivers. It is still possible however to motor safely on the road at speeds of more than 100 m.p.h., provided one picks the right moment and a good car.

One model I would choose for this kind of motoring is the Continental Bentley, one of the fastest, safe, luxury vehicles in the world, in the hands of an experienced driver. It provides the type of motoring most of us dream about, with a maximum speed in excess of 120 m.p.h., good handling characteristics throughout its range and enough acceleration to quietly dispose of most cars as though they were motionless. But to my mind one of its greatest charms is the complete absence of noise and fuss that so often has to be endured in a car possessed of tremendous performance.

This, of course, is in marked contrast to its immortal ancestors, those famous Bentleys which dominated Le Mans and other great races, machines that really established the legend of the British sports car. The latest model offers a ride and comfort undreamed of by that earlier, tough generation, who drove those hard-riding, thunderous Bentleys fast for the sheer hell of it. If only Ettore Bugatti were alive today, no longer would the great man refer to the modern Bentley Speed Model as the fastest lorry in the world.

To enjoy really high speed motoring over deserted roads nowadays, one needs to get up very early in the morning, but this I found no particular hardship with a Continental Bentley awaiting my pleasure. Indeed, what can be more delightful to the keen driver on a spring morning, just as dawn is breaking, than to move swiftly and silently over empty roads with the thrilling anticipation of driving a magnificent thoroughbred really quickly.

Along fast highways 100 m.p.h. comes up very quickly indeed, and gives no more sensation than 70 m.p.h. on the average fast machine. It is pleasant to be able to feel the wheels in contact with the roads, to know what the front end is doing. On this machine a certain amount of feed-back

CONTINENTAL

by JERRY AMES

through the steering is noticeable, perhaps slightly more than one expects at high speeds, but the steering is beautifully precise. At lower speeds there is a slight trace of understeer, but this vanishes as one gets into the higher speed ranges.

I found the steering to be without any vices and it is possible to take known bends a great deal more quickly and safely than on the average fast car. Early in the morning several fast curves were taken in the region of 100 m.p.h. without any anxiety at all.

When fast cornering is indulged in, the car is pleasantly free from roll, especially if the switch near the facia controlling the rear dampers is moved over to "hard". The front end always feels in one piece with the rest of the car and this is particularly noticeable coming out of more acute corners under full power when there is no front end patter nor any tyre noise, unless one allows the back end to break away, under these circumstances the car can be easily controlled.

Fastest model in the Bentley range is appreciably lighter than standard, in fact a weight saving of some four cwt. has been achieved on this superb Park Ward coupé. Only a few modifications have been made to the 4.9-litre engine, which otherwise follows current Bentley design, with overhead inlet and side exhaust valves. On the Continental, two huge S.U. carburetters feed the mixture through to larger valves, closed by springs stronger than those used on the touring car. For many years mixture has been compressed at 8 to 1, in combustion chambers noted for promoting an excellent degree of turbulence, although this compression ratio has now been standardized on the slower models, the manufacturers have wisely left well alone on the Continental, preferring not to sacrifice the wonderful smoothness for higher performance. In any case this engine produces ample power (not disclosed in accordance with the firm's policy), for fast motoring on the road.

The Continental under test was fitted with the extremely efficient Rolls-Royce fully automatic transmission, comprising a four-speed gearbox driven by a fluid coupling. Before any of the old school Bentley Drivers Club members choke themselves to death at the very thought of an automatic transmission on their most esteemed motor car, let me hasten to assure them that Bentley engineers like to make their own gear changes too, and so they have provided an over-riding manual control. Therefore, if you wish to make your own gear changes you can do so, but if you feel lazy, place the gear lever in fourth position and this work is all done for you.

Drive is continued by an open propellor shaft divided and supported in the centre by a flexibly mounted ball race, the rear axle is of the semi-floating type and the final drive is through hypoid bevel gears, offset to provide a low body position without sacrificing ground clearance. Large helical springs enclosing hydraulic dampers, together with an anti-roll bar take care of the front suspension, whilst semi-elliptic leaf springs are used at the rear. Some adjustment to the rear dampers by means of a switch below the steering wheel gives the driver a measure of extra control over the back end. The strong box-section chassis is rigidly braced and accounts for a great deal of the solidity of the Continental. Gear ratios are higher that the standard "S" series, but the faster model pulls them with ease.

Another feature new to the Continental is power steering, available only as an optional extra for those who prefer it. Personally I don't care for it on a very fast car, however good it may be, and was therefore delighted to discover this

With the hood erected the coachwork line is still neat and unfussy. A large car, 17 ft. 6½ in. long and 6 ft. wide the Continental is easy to handle at speed. Really large doors permit easy access to rear seat

form of assistance had been omitted on the test coupé. One does not need the strength of a Samson to turn the Bentley wheel, the steering is surprisingly light for such a large and heavy car; after taking a corner the wheel spins easily back with just the right amount of self-centring action. I will concede that ladies might find the steering a mite heavy when parking in a fairly tight space.

For continuous fast motoring, the pressure of the India Super Speed Special tyres should be increased from the normal 22/24 lb. to 30/35; this of course gives a harder but safer ride at speed and brings to light one or two rattles one does not otherwise hear. Incidentally the excellent Park Ward Coupé body was absolutely silent when normal tyre pressures were used.

The last Continental I drove had a manual synchromesh gearbox and I was able to exceed 100 m.p.h. on third, but maximum speed in this gear on the current model proved to be 78 m.p.h. Curiously enough with the present transmission this did not seem to be a real disadvantage, for the acceleration was all that one needed, although I felt that second gear with its maximum of 46 m.p.h. could have been a little higher with advantage.

This fully automatic transmission is one of the smoothest in the world, even when the "kick-down" is employed to engage a lower gear, it is practically free from the customary

The six-cylinder i.o.e. engine propels the Continental at 100 m.p.h. plus, in silence and without effort. Finished in black enamel the engine and engine compartment is a joy to behold, there were no oil leaks. Twin S.U. carburetters are fitted and there are six separate inlet ports

Specification

PERFORMANCE

0 to 30 m.p.h.	..	..	3.4 sec.
0 to 40 m.p.h.	..	..	6.1 sec.
0 to 50 m.p.h.	..	..	8.2 sec.
0 to 60 m.p.h.	..	..	10.8 sec.
0 to 70 m.p.h.	..	..	13.6 sec.
0 to 80 m.p.h.	..	..	17.2 sec.
0 to 90 m.p.h.	..	..	24.6 sec.
0 to 100 m.p.h.	..	..	34.1 sec.

Maximum speed:

Top	..	..	122.4 m.p.h.
3rd	..	..	78.0 m.p.h.
2nd ..	..	..	46.0 m.p.h.
1st	..	..	23.0 m.p.h.

Fuel consumption: normal, 17 to 18 m.p.g.; driven hard, 15 m.p.g.

ENGINE

6-cylinder. Bore: 95.25. Stroke: 114.3 mm. Capacity: 4,887 c.c. Overhead inlet, side exhaust valves. Compression ratio 8 : 1. Twin S.U. carburetters.

TRANSMISSION

Fully automatic with fluid coupling and Rolls-Royce epicyclic gearbox. Overriding manual control. Ratios: 2.92, 4.25, 7.69, 11.17. Hypoid bevel final drive.

SUSPENSION

Front: independent by coil springs, wishbones and anti-roll bar. Rear: semi-elliptic springs. Double acting piston type dampers, adjustable at rear by switch below steering wheel.

STEERING

Cam and roller steering (power assistance available as optional extra). Turning circle 41 ft. (4½ turns lock to lock).

BRAKES

Hydraulic brakes with mechanical servo.

DIMENSIONS

Wheelbase 10 ft. 3 in. Track (front) 4 ft. 10 in. Track (rear): 5 ft. Overall length: 17 ft. 6½ in. Overall width: 6 ft. Overall height: 5 ft. 2½ in. Ground clearance: 7 in. Kerb weight: 35 cwt.

TANK CAPACITY

Fuel tank capacity 18 gallons.

PRICE

With Park Ward Drop-head coupé as tested. Basic £4,995. Purchase tax £2,498 17s. Total £7493 17s.

jerk. No clutch pedal is provided and normally one motors all the time with the gear in fourth position. But a manual over-riding control permits the lower gears to be engaged just by moving the gear lever into one of the other notches on the quadrant, thus the enthusiastic driver trained in the use of the old-fashioned crash box will find the Bentley automatic transmission quite acceptable.

Ignoring the automatic transmission and using the gears in the ordinary way, acceleration can be rather shattering for such a heavy, luxurious car; the Continental Bentley soon showed itself able to whip past production sports cars with an ease that is most deceptive. This is indeed the model *par excellence* for high speed cruising, on fast roads one can keep the speedometer needle continuously between 90 and 100 m.p.h.

With the tyres at normal road pressures the ride is extremely comfortable, if additional damping is required the ride-control below the wheel can be moved over to "H" when the rear dampers will be hardened, but this is not usually needed unless one intends to drive quickly.

Good brakes are of first importance on a fast car and Bentley mechanical servo brakes are as good as you will find on any road machine equipped with drums. They can be used often at speeds of more that 100 m.p.h. without inducing fade, nor do they lose their wonderful smoothness and effective stopping power, only light pedal pressure is needed. A dry disc type servo is employed, driven by the gearbox; the front brakes are operated entirely by hydraulic pressure, but the rear brakes, hydraulically and mechanically by servo simultaneously, in the proportion of 60 per cent hydraulic and 40 per cent mechanical.

The twist and pull handbrake under the facia works on the rear brakes only and uses part of the foot pedal linkage—it is most effective.

A good driving position is essential in a fast car and in this respect the Bentley excels, the soft well-sprung individual leather covered seats give correct support in the right places and the well padded backs can be altered for rake. There is a generous fore and aft adjustment of both seats and between them is a dividing arm-rest, that lifts up to reveal a useful tray below. In the rear seats there is more than average leg room for a close-coupled coupé and of course absolute luxury, armrests are fitted on the sides for each occupant, those in the front being adjustable, whilst ash trays are always within easy reach.

Despite a long bonnet forward visibility is excellent, both front wings can be seen, enabling the car to be aimed accurately at speed, or when manoeuvring in traffic; hind visibility is aided by a fairly large rear window, but of course one has the usual drophead coupé blind spots on the quarters, therefore some caution is needed when turning into a main stream of traffic. I found the very full range of instruments rather well sited, the large 140 m.p.h. speedometer and the rev. counter reading to 5,000 r.p.m. could be quite easily noted when motoring quickly.

An elaborate hot and cold air system enables one to maintain a comfortable temperature. Very efficient de-misting is also provided. The large three-spoke steering wheel is nicely raked and all the essential controls are well positioned; by pressing the two-speed wiper control a screen wash is brought into action. A green warning light flashes when the petrol level is down to three gallons, the flap to the filler of the 18 gallon tank is unlocked by a lever on the facia, this did not always work and then one had to resort to a hand attachment in the boot.

At speed the hood remains taut and with the windows closed there are no draughts, the hood can be folded neatly and quickly and covered by a special bag. The unusual shape of the boot interior is deceptive, nevertheless a very large quantity of luggage can be carried; tools and spare wheel are stored in this compartment, but in their own lockers and therefore do not come into contact with any baggage. Although the headlamps are excellent for fast driving at night, when dipped they are a little disappointing and speed needs to be considerably curtailed. Maintenance is kept to

Extremely comfortable seats are adjustable for rake as well as for to and fro movement. Walnut facia is in true Bentley tradition and still retains the white figures on round, black dial instruments. Steering column mounted lever provides overriding control for the automatic transmission

The floor of the enormous boot is covered with carpet. Tools and spare wheel are under covers. Rear lighting is small but adequate, rear lights with separate reflectors. Top lamps are direction indicators

an absolute minimum by the excellent one-shot lubrication system, a pedal under the facia merely needs pumping every 200 miles, apart from this two grease nipples on the propellor shaft require attention from a gun every 10,000 miles. Fuel consumption for such a very fast machine is extremely good, when driven really hard one can expect a figure around 15 m.p.g. but under more normal driving this improves to 17 to 18 m.p.g.

In an expensive motor car one naturally expects standards approaching perfection. So well designed and finished is the Continental Bentley that even after several hundred miles at the wheel one has little but praise for its construction and handling. It is without question one of the most desirable fast machines in the world, but like everything built regardless of cost the price of the finished car unfortunately places it out of the reach of all but the most wealthy drivers. ★

BOOKS

AUTO PARADE: Published by Arthur Logoz, of Zurich. Obtainable from the sole U.K. distributors, Motor Books, 41/42 Parliament Street, Whitehall, London S.W.1. Price 3 gns. nett.

Quite one of the most complete, and certainly the most lavish automobile catalogue to be published, Auto-Parade contains 290 large pages impeccably printed in the Swiss manner. It is a complete international reference which not only deals with virtually every current production car in the world, but also has a lengthy specification panel on each model in six languages—English, German, French, Italian, Spanish and Portuguese.

Outstanding models have a three-language (English, German and French) description in addition to technical data, but the most outstanding feature of this noteworthy tome is the fact that every one of the 297 illustrations is printed in full colour. Even the latest Russian, Czech and Japanese cars are included in the book, and it is up-to-date enough to cover Lotus Elite, Vespa, Edsel, Saab Sonett, etc. With this annual on his shelf, the enthusiast can check details and prove arguments on practically any car.—D.A.

GREAT MOMENTS IN MOTORING, by Phil Drackett: Published by Phoenix House Ltd., 38 William IV Street, Charing Cross, London, W.C.2. Price 7s. 6d. nett.

Phil Drackett has written several books on motoring subjects and all can be said to represent a worthy addition to motoring literature. In his latest book *"Great Moments"* he covers ten chapters of outstanding happenings in sport and history. The eleventh chapter deals with the "Car of Tomorrow", and deals with the exciting record run by the Rover Company's turbine car JET I. in 1950.

As a condensed history of motoring sport at a low price *"Great Moments"* is hard to beat on a value for money basis. It starts with the story of Austrian motoring pioneer Siegfried Marcus, and other early automobilists, and travels to the 20th century with stories of the ill-fated Paris-Madrid race, Henry Ford's "Tin Lizzie", Frank Lockhart's amazing Stutz Blackhawk, and Mike Hawthorn's colossal struggle (and victory) against Juan Fangio in the 1953 French Grand Prix at Rheims. Truly great moments. The drawings are first-class.—D.A.

SPEED AND A MICROPHONE, by Robin Richards: Published by William Kimber and Co. Ltd., 46 Wilton Place, London, S.W.1. Price 21s. nett.

Robin Richards, the well-known B.B.C. motoring commentator, and erstwhile race and rally commentator is well qualified to write a book about the Sport, but he has mercifully avoided falling into the groove of uninteresting subjects which seems to be the current trend. Instead he has rendered a real service to motoring sport by setting out to "educate" the man-in-the-street into the intricacies of all categories of this nowadays highly involved subject.

has two master cylinders plus a mechanical hook-up to the rear shoes. Failure is thus impossible. Also notable are the Z-member, which eliminates bouncing of the rear wheels, and the special floating centre bearing of the divided propeller shaft, which avoids vibration and snatch in the transmission.

When one enters the Bentley, a sense of well-being is at once engendered. The sheer quality of the polished wood, the leather upholstery, and the head lining and carpets, is something that no other car can approach. The all-round visibility is excellent, and although this is a very big car, quite a large proportion of it is ahead of the driver. Personally, I would prefer an old-fashioned lever to the pull-out hand brake.

The automatic transmission has the

THE BENTLEY CONTINENTAL

THE Rolls-Royce and Bentley cars of the current "S-series" combine high performance with luxury in an astonishing manner. These machines now have the high-compression engine that was originally a "Continental" feature, and are capable of speeds around 105 m.p.h., coupled with outstanding acceleration.

Nevertheless, it was found that a demand existed for a Continental version of the new car. This model has now been introduced, and I have recently been able to try one over quite a useful mileage. The theory behind the Continental is that, by reducing the frontal area and the weight, the 4.9-litre engine will pull an axle ratio of 2.92:1, against 3.42:1 for the Standard S-series. This change increases the maximum speed by a full 10 m.p.h. Furthermore, a different governor setting is employed for the automatic gearbox, which enables the driver to run up to a maximum speed of 82 m.p.h. in third gear, as opposed to 67 m.p.h. or so.

Naturally, much of the extra performance is due to the design of the body. The test car was fitted with a Mulliner two-door saloon of light alloy construction. The front seats are special lightweight ones, with adjustable backs which can be folded down for access to the rear seat. This is a bench-type, with folding central arm rest. The luggage boot is of fair size, but the swept tail shape limits its vertical dimension.

The engine is the well-known big six, with inlet valves seating in the head and exhaust valves in the block. It is rubber mounted at three points, and assembled in unit with the four-speed automatic gearbox and fluid clutch. The driver may over-ride the automatic selection by using the hand-lever, with the exception that the governor prevents destructive over-revving of the engine. For instance, if he attempts to change down at 100 m.p.h., the transmission will hold the direct drive until the speed has been reduced to 80 m.p.h. or so. There is a "kick-down" on the accelerator.

There are three notable features about the otherwise conventional chassis. The most important of these is the servo-brake system, which includes the famous Rolls-Royce gearbox-driven servo, and

unusual virtue of being entirely free from "creep", even when starting from cold. The big machine may be eased away almost imperceptibly from a standstill, and it will float along at 30 m.p.h. in top gear with the rev. counter in the region of 1,000 r.p.m. Alternatively, firm pressure on the accelerator will produce two black lines on the tarmac, under which conditions the mighty torque of those great cylinders results in really spectacular acceleration.

The high gearing of the Continental makes it a little less lively on top speed than the standard model, but the increased revolution range in third gear more than makes up for this. Quite apart from performance figures, the untiring ease of fast travel with the engine turning relatively slowly is one of those intangibles that render the Continental ideal for long distance touring. The change, either up or down, between top and third gears is barely perceptible, but the wider gap between third and second occasionally makes itself felt. At the timed maximum speed of 115.4 m.p.h., the rev. counter indicated 4,000 r.p.m.

POWER UNIT (left). The well-known big six, with inlet valves seating in the head and exhaust valves in the block, is rubber mounted at three points and assembled with the four-speed automatic gearbox and fluid clutch. The luggage boot (right) is of fair size but the swept tail shape limits its vertical dimension.

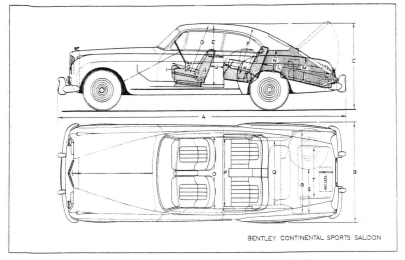

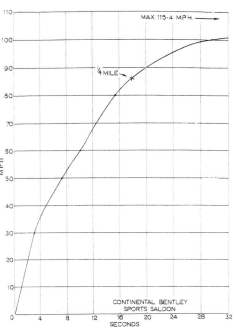

Bentley Continental Sports Saloon

A Overall length, 17 ft. 8 ins.
B Overall width, 5 ft. 11½ ins.
C Overall height, 5 ft. 2 ins.
D Front seat head room, 3 ft. 1 in.
E Floor to roof, 3 ft. 7½ ins.
F Rear seat head room, 2 ft. 10½ ins.
G Depth of front seat cushion, 1 ft. 8½ ins.
H Steering wheel to seat squab, 1 ft. 0½ ins.
I Steering wheel to seat cushion, 6 ins.
J Back of front seat to edge of rear seat cushion, 9½ ins.
K Depth of rear seat cushion, 1 ft. 8 ins.
L Depth of luggage compartment, 4 ft. 1 in.

M Height of luggage compartment, 1 ft. 4 ins.
N Height at front end of luggage compartment, 1 ft. 3 ins.
O Width between doors at belt, 4 ft. 4 ins.
P Width of rear seat between arm rests, 4 ft. 0 in.
Q Width of luggage compartment between wheel arches, 3 ft. 10 ins.
R Width of luggage compartment, 4 ft. 10 ins.
S Width of luggage compartment between side and spare wheel, 2 ft. 6 ins.
T Width of luggage compartment door opening, 2 ft. 11 ins.

Acceleration Graph

It is a pleasure once again to be able to praise the brakes of the Bentley. The largest American cars may be able to compete with it in sheer speed, but their brakes are not in the same world. There is a smell of hot linings after repeated high speed applications, but no reasonable driver will experience brake fade.

Considering its large size and substantial weight, the car handles well. It remains controllable at high speeds on wet roads, and in this respect it is infinitely better than the Bentleys of a few years ago. If one drives too fast on really bad roads, one becomes conscious that the suspension is hitting on the bump stops, but under all normal conditions the ride is as luxurious as one would expect.

With its good roadholding and brakes, and with really fierce acceleration available at a touch of the pedal, one naturally drives this car fast. Given a clear road, 100 m.p.h. is as good a cruising speed as any other, and the miles, or kilometres, are swallowed up as the passengers relax in comfort. On some of our winding roads, a large car is at a disadvantage, but it is a compliment to say that the Bentley's size is not so apparent as one would expect.

The Bentley Continental is a car of severely classical design which nevertheless achieves a high degree of excellence by sheer quality of construction. In doing so, it develops an individuality, a character, call it what you will, that makes it entirely different from any other *marque*. The man who drives a Continental lives in an enchanted world, for everybody calls him "sir" and he may park where lesser cars can never tread. I have never met so many polite policemen as when I was driving this Bentley!

SPECIFICATION AND PERFORMANCE DATA

Car Tested: Bentley Continental two-door Mulliner saloon. Price £5,275 (£7,913 17s. including P.T.).
Engine: Six cylinders 95.25 mm. x 114.30 mm. (4,887 c.c.). Overhead inlet and side exhaust valves. Compression ratio 8 to 1. Twin SU carburetters with automatic choke. Delco-Remy twin contact breaker distributor.
Transmission: Fluid clutch and four-speed epicyclic gearbox with automatic change, plus over-riding hand control and kick-down. Ratios: 2.92, 4.25, 7.69, and 11.17 to 1. Open divided propeller shaft with floating steady bearing. Hypoid rear axle.
Chassis: Box section frame with cruciform bracing. Independent front suspension by wishbones and helical springs. Cam and roller steering box connected by transverse link to three-piece track rod. Rear axle on semi-elliptic springs with combined torque-resisting and anti-roll member. Piston-type dampers all round, with two-position electric control at rear. 8.00-15 ins. tyres on five-stud disc wheels. Hydraulic brakes in front, with hydrostatic non-adjustable shoes, operated by gearbox-driven mechanical servo. Rear brakes 60 per cent. hydraulically operated by servo and 40 per cent. mechanically direct from pedal. Separate master cylinders and reservoirs for front and rear brakes. Pull-out hand brake on rear wheels. 11¼ ins. x 3 ins. finned cast iron drums all round.
Equipment: 12-volt lighting and starting. Speedometer. Rev. counter. Ammeter. Oil pressure, water temperature, petrol and sump level gauges with warning light. Two-speed self-parking windscreen wipers and washers. Flashing direction indicators. Cigar lighter. Built-in heating, demisting, and ventilation system. Clock, radio, spotlights, picnic tables. Ladies' companions.
Dimensions: Wheelbase, 10 ft. 3 ins.; track, front 4 ft. 10 ins. rear 5 ft.; overall length, 17 ft. 8 ins.; width, 5 ft. 11½ ins. Turning circle, 41 ft. 8 ins. Weight, 1 ton 15 cwt. (approx.).
Performance: Maximum speed, 115.4 m.p.h. Standing quarter-mile, 17.8 secs. Acceleration: 0-30 m.p.h. 3 secs.; 0-50 m.p.h. 7.2 secs.; 0-60 m.p.h. 10.2 secs.; 0-80 m.p.h. 15.4 secs.; 0-100 m.p.h. 29.6 secs.
Fuel Consumption: 14 m.p.g.

DASHBOARD LAYOUT in the Bentley style. The big steering wheel, large instruments and fine quality panelling are well shown.

Bentley
TURBO RT

MODEL TESTED Turbo RT **ON-ROAD PRICE** £148,990
TOP SPEED 152mph **0-60MPH** 6.7sec **30-70MPH** 6.1sec
60-0MPH 3.0sec **MPG** 13.3 **FIRST TEST** 23.11.88 (Turbo R)
FOR Huge performance, unbeatable interior, a real Bentley
AGAINST Absurd fuel consumption, outdated dynamics

Just when you thought it was safe to go back on the roads, Bentley has unleashed its biggest, fastest, most expensive road saloon ever. The Turbo RT is the latest (and probably last) evolution of the model which has served as its front-line saloon since 1985. In 2000 an all-new car with BMW V12 power will lay these bones to rest.

In the meantime, sit back and try to digest some of the most amazing statistics you'll ever set eyes upon in a road test. The Turbo RT is 17.6ft long, weighs 2476kg, costs £148,990 and is powered by a turbocharged 6.75-litre V8 engine with 400bhp, 590lb ft

and the ability to burn fuel at 5.1mpg. This should give you some idea of just how serious a machine the Turbo RT is.

Conceived as a replacement for the original Turbo R, the new RT is distinguished by its body-coloured bumpers, traditional wire mesh grille, five-spoke alloy wheels and the engine and drivetrain from last year's Continental T coupe.

A remapped Zytek management system allows the two Garrett T2 turbochargers to force the fuel/air mixture into the engine at up to 0.76bar, boosting the naturally aspirated output from 246bhp up to 400bhp at 4000rpm. This in

Mesh grille makes a comeback

Torquiest engine in the world

itself is achievement enough and puts the Bentley on bed-sharing terms with the 408bhp Mercedes S600, but take into account the RT's 590lb ft of torque (produced between 2000 and 3450rpm) and even the big Merc's 427lb ft is made to look puny. Put simply, the RT is the torquiest production car in the world, bar none.

Press the big drilled throttle pedal in any gear and a barely audible rumble like the thunder from some distant storm cloud forewarns you of the coming deluge. Fractions of a second later the monster surges forward with such smooth,

relentless pace that the whole experience takes on a strangel[y] surreal edge. Only the steady progress of the needle arcing i[ts] way around the old-fashioned white-on-black speedometer brings you back to reality and the imminent threat hanging over your driving licence.

In scientific terms, the Bentley thunders its way from rest to 60mph in 6.7sec, reache[s] 100mph just 10.2sec later and doesn't give up until the needl[e] is wedged firm at a perfectly accurate 152mph. This would not be so surprising if it were a[?] lightweight two-seat sports ca[r] but the fact that all these

:clining seats, champagne fridge, video. What more could you want?

figures were recorded on a computer by a road tester sitting in the back seat surrounded by two televisions, a video player, champagne cooler and enough wood and leather to make the palace of Versailles look restrained, speaks for itself.

The only reason it's not any faster through the gears than the previous Turbo R we tested in 1988 is down to the copious extra equipment, which pushes the weight up from an already portly 2245kg to a scarcely believable 2476kg. Bear in mind that the heaviest Range Rover 4.6 HSE tips the scales at 2049kg and you should get

some idea of the forces at work. This is the reason why we were unable to better 13.3mpg during average motoring and 16.5mpg over our gentle touring route. It also smashed our existing record low by gulping down a gallon every 5.1 miles during performance testing.

The GM-sourced four-speed automatic gearbox uses dynamic shift pattern processing to vary the change-up points according to driving style, although a small switch on the lever allows you to manually select the quickest sports mode. It is not quite as smooth as the best five-speed ▶

35

ENGINE

Layout 8 cyls in vee, 6750cc
Max power 400bhp at 4000rpm
Max torque 590lb ft at 2000-3450rpm
Specific output 59bhp per litre
Power to weight 162bhp per tonne
Torque to weight 238lb ft per tonne
Installation front, longitudinal, rear-wheel drive
Construction alloy head, iron block
Bore/stroke 104/99mm
Valve gear 2 valves per cyl, ohv
Compression ratio 8.0:1
Ignition and fuel Zytek engine management system controlling Garrett T2 turbocharger

GEARBOX

Type 4-speed auto
Ratios/mph per 1000rpm
1st 2.48/12.5 **2nd** 1.48/20.2
3rd 1.00/30.0 **4th** 0.75/40.0
Final drive ratio 2.69:1

MAXIMUM SPEEDS

4th 152/3800 **3rd** 135/4000
2nd 90/4500 **1st** 56/4000

ACCELERATION FROM REST

True mph	sec	speedo mph
30	2.4	30
40	3.5	40
50	4.8	50
60	6.7	60
70	8.5	70
80	10.6	80
90	13.5	90
100	16.9	100
110	20.8	110
120	26.2	120
130	34.3	130

Standing qtr mile 15.0sec/94mph
Standing kilo 26.8sec/121mph
30-70mph in kickdown 6.1sec

ACCELERATION IN KICKDOWN

mph	sec
20-40	1.9
30-50	2.4
40-60	3.2
50-70	3.7
60-80	4.0
70-90	5.0
80-110	6.2
90-110	7.3
100-120	9.3
110-130	13.5

STEERING

Type Rack and pinion, power assisted
Turns lock to lock 3.3

CONTROLS IN DETAIL

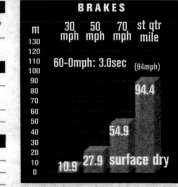

1 Four-speed auto gearbox has intelligent shift patterns and sports mode
2 Climate control eshews digital panel in favour of two split-level chrome wheels 3 Alpine stereo hides behind wood panel, CD changer in the centre console 4 Each chromed eyeball vent has its own organ stop to control the airflow 5 Row of dials include boost gauge and fuel gauge that doubles as an oil level check 6 Electronic panel gives digital readouts of faults

SUSPENSION

Front Struts, lower wishbones, coils, electronic dampers, anti-roll bar
Rear Trailing arms, coils, electronic dampers, anti-roll bar

WHEELS & TYRES

Wheel size 7.5Jx17in
Made of Cast alloy **Tyres** 255/55 WR17 Avon turbospeed
Spare Full size

BRAKES

Front 340mm ventilated discs
Rear 277mm discs
Anti-lock standard

BRAKES

m	30 mph	50 mph	70 mph	st qtr mile
60-0mph: 3.0sec	(94mph)			

60-0mph: 3.0sec (94mph)
94.4
54.9
10.9 27.9 surface dry

GEARING

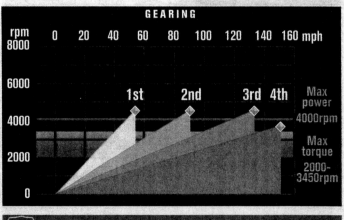

AUTOCAR road tests are conducted using BP Unleaded or BP Diesel Plus with additives to help keep engines cleaner

TEST RESULTS

FUEL CONSUMPTION

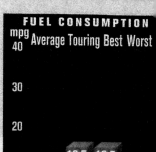

mpg — Average Touring Best Worst
13.3 16.5 16.5 5.1

GOVERNMENT CLAIMS

mpg	Urban	Extra urban	Combined
	11.0	21.2	15.9

Tank capacity: 109 litres (24 gallon)
Touring range: 396 miles

NOISE

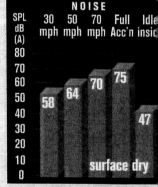

SPL dB (A) — 30 mph 50 mph 70 mph Full Acc'n Idle insid
58 64 70 75 47
surface dry

LAYOUT

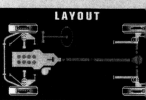

Body 4dr saloon **Cd** na **Front/rear tracks** 1549/1549mm **Turning circle** 12.6m **Min/max front leg room** 900/1070mm **Min/max rear leg room** 710/915mm **Min/max front head room** 850/900mm **Rear head room** 880mm **Interior width front/rear** 1525/1535mm **Boot length/width/hei** 800/1300/420mm **VDA boot volume** 350 litres/dm3 **Kerb weight** 2476kg **Distribution f/r** 53/47 per cent **Max payload** 500kg **Max towing weig**

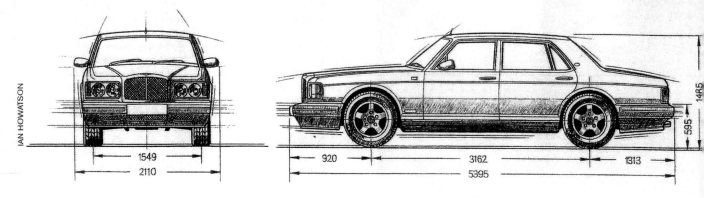

IAN HOWATSON

1549
2110
920 3162 1313
5395
1485
595

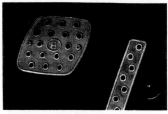

New five-spoke 17in sports alloys

Weight-saving drilled pedals. Not

Electronically controlled dampers do their best to keep body movements under control; better in a straight line

automatics, but with such a broad spread of torque and widely spaced gears this could hardly be described as problematic. If anything, it could be lazier still to prevent the occasional kickdown midway through a corner.

The twin-caliper anti-lock brakes which disperse all this energy do a fine job of scrubbing off speed without the previous model's tendency to overheat and fade, but the dive under braking and sensitive pedal make it hard not to send the passenger's drinks sliding into the footwell.

Computer-controlled dampers working off lever arm front suspension and trailing arms with a Panhard rod at the rear help to disguise the chassis' age. At speed they deliver an amazingly stable ride with excellent straight-line body

control. Small dips and crests are crushed out of existence, although certain relatively minor intrusions such as drain covers, motorway joints and cat's eyes do upset the cabin's usual serenity.

Introduce corners into the equation and the outcome is even less civilised. Traction control stops things getting too far out of shape, but the tall tyre walls, lack of roll control and unusually flexible chassis make hard cornering an unsettling experience for everyone bar the driver. Not only is he better located, thanks to the support of a chunky four-spoke steering wheel and a supremely comfortable chair, but he is also aware that, despite the audible protests from rubber, steel, leather and assorted passengers, the Bentley Turbo RT is still

capable of cornering at an indecent pace.

As with any other Rolls-Royce product, the RT's true forte is its cabin. Opulent doesn't begin to describe such a homage to hedonism, even if the crushed raspberry colour scheme isn't entirely to our taste. You sit way up high on a pile of Connolly's finest and inch-thick lamb's wool rugs, looking down on the stream of mass market tin boxes below. The rows of chrome-rimmed instruments (including a wonderfully inappropriate boost gauge) remind you that this is no ordinary motor car. Even the indicator stalk feels different due to its cool-to-the-touch bakelite construction and absurdly long travel.

For the full experience, however, you have to sit in the back, where the copious

options ranging from the refrigerated drinks cooler (£4406) to the twin video monitors (£6456) and cocktail cabinets (£3871) transform the longest journeys into a travelling experience without equal. You can even spend up to £3500 on extras for the boot, such as fitted umbrellas.

It is this made-to-measure feel that justifies the Bentley's price. If truth be told, it is no longer as refined, comfortable, economical or competent as its vastly cheaper rivals from Mercedes, BMW, Jaguar and the like. What it is, is infinitely more special. It takes a certain type of person to carry it off with conviction, but if you can afford a Bentley Turbo RT and are entertained by the absurdity of its performance, it's an experience that you should not deny yourself.

WHAT IT COSTS

On-road price	£148,990
Total as tested	£163,723
Cost per mile	n/a

EQUIPMENT
(bold = options fitted to test car)

Automatic transmission	●
Cruise control	●
Airbag driver/passenger	●/●
Heated/memory front seats	●/●
ABS brakes/traction control	●/●
Alarm/immobiliser	●/●
RDS stereo/CD player	●/●
Televison/video	**£6456**
Leather trim/air con	●/●
Electric tilt steering column	●
GSM telephone	●
Heated rear seats	**£557**
Champagne fridge	**£4406**
Cocktail cabinets	**£3871**
● standard	
Insurance group	20

WARRANTY
3 years unconditional

SERVICING
Major 15,000 miles
Interim 7500 miles

RT can corner hard, but not without protest from tyres, chassis and passengers

The ultimate luxury bruiser ★★★

Bentley ARNAGE

MODEL TESTED Arnage **ON-ROAD PRICE** £145,000
TOP SPEED 150mph **0-60MPH** 6.3sec
30-70MPH 5.7sec **60-0MPH** 3.2sec **MPG** 13.7mpg
FOR Seductive performance, beautifully built, smooth gearchange
AGAINST Huge thirst, reduced rear leg room, price beside S-class

A more special new arrival is difficult to imagine. The launch of a brand new Bentley is something connoisseurs of the marque have been waiting for with baited breath. A Rolls-Royce might still represent the ultimate expression of wealth for some, but these days more people buy Bentleys.

Somewhat poignantly, this version of the all-new Arnage (named after a corner at Le Mans) already has its days numbered. Since the sale of Rolls-Royce to Volkswagen, doubt has surrounded the involvement of rival bidder and engine supplier BMW. The most likely outcome is that BMW will honour its one-year supply contract, but not renew it. As those at the Crewe factory cheerfully point out, this car could be the best engineered special edition in the history of the automobile. As for the nomenclature of a replacement VW engine, watch this space.

In the meantime, a full 12 months of BMW power is in the offing. We've already witnessed the effect of the Munich manufacturer on Rolls-Royce's Silver Seraph. For the most part it has been a positive one. Mind you, the Arnage is no rebadged Seraph. Despite its similar external appearance, it is a thoroughly different car. Powering the huge saloon is a 4.4-litre V8, as used in the BMW 740i (the Seraph has a 5.4-litre V12). As has become traditional for the Bentley marque recently, the £145,000 Arnage is turbocharged, in this instance via a pair of Cosworth-engineered Garrett blowers.

Power spirals to 350bhp, 64bhp up on the regular V8, while torque peaks at 413lb ft between 2500 and 4200rpm. Both figures are some way down on the previous Turbo

Mesh radiator grille equals Arnage

TOM SALT

RT, whose 400bhp and 590lb ft were record numbers for Bentley. Offsetting the relative lack of muscle is an electronic five-speed automatic gearbox (one cog more than the RT) and a kerb weight of 2330kg, some 146kg lighter than before.

Externally, many small changes distinguish the Bentley from the Seraph. There are deeper bumpers front and rear and body-coloured wing mirrors, plus a wire mesh grille. Partial dechroming around the rear number plate is another giveaway. And the Arnage rides on five-spoke alloy wheels with 255/55 WR17 Avon Turbospeed tyres, which give the Bentley a more aggressive stance.

Inside, a wealth of style

Ride is firmer, less soothing than RR equivalent, especially in town. But handling is sharper and more controlled

Door handles are carried over; BMW 4.4 V8 has twin turbos and 350bhp

changes give the Arnage its own identity. Extra dials in the middle of the dash are an obvious addition. Oil pressure, water temperature and battery level gauges join the clock and fuel gauge. A tachometer is included as well, next to the equally large speedometer. The gear selector is located between the front seats (rather than on the steering column) and bespoke seats with extra side bolstering are unique to the Arnage. On a long journey they are supremely comfortable, providing peerless support.

At first the driving position feels a little too stately for a car of the Arnage's sporting pretensions, but as the miles roll on it quickly becomes more acceptable. A commanding view of the road is a real benefit, especially considering the size of the car. And then, of course, there's the performance.

Broadly speaking, the Arnage performs slightly better than the Turbo RT. It thunders to 60mph in 6.3sec and cracks 100mph in 15.9sec (RT 6.7sec, 16.9sec). By any standards, this is a rapid machine. Top speed is limited to 150mph.

Considering the magnitude of the performance, we were left a little disappointed by the brakes. The ventilated discs faded badly during repeated hard usage and pedal feel itself was spongey. Even during light braking the initial bite was not as good as we'd expected, ◗

ENGINE

Layout 8 cyls in 90deg vee, 4398cc
Max power 350bhp at 5500rpm
Max torque 413lb ft from 2500-4200rpm
Specific output 80bhp per litre
Power to weight 150bhp per tonne
Torque to weight 177lb ft per tonne
Installation Front, longitudinal, rear-wheel drive
Construction Alloy heads and block
Bore/stroke 92.0/79.0mm
Valve gear 4 valves per cyl, dohc per bank
Compression ratio 8.5:1
Ignition and fuel Bosch M5.2.1 engine management, twin Garrett turbochargers

GEARBOX

Type 5-speed automatic by ZF
Ratios/mph per 1000rpm
1st 3.55/8.0 **2nd** 2.24/12.7 **3rd** 1.54/18.5
4th 1.00/28.5 **5th** 0.79/36.0
Final drive ratio 2.93:1

MAXIMUM SPEEDS

5th 150mph/4160rpm **4th** 150/5260rpm
3rd 116/6250 **2nd** 79/6250 **1st** 50/6250

ACCELERATION FROM REST

True mph	sec	speedo mph
30	2.5	31
40	3.4	41
50	4.8	52
60	6.3	62
70	8.1	72
80	10.3	82
90	12.9	92
100	15.9	102

Standing qtr mile 14.9sec/96mph
Standing km 26.5sec/122mph
30-70mph through gears 5.7sec

ACCELERATION IN K'DOWN

mph	sec	gear
10-30	1.5	1st
20-40	1.5	1st
30-50	2.3	1st
40-60	2.9	1st/2nd
50-70	3.4	2nd
60-80	4.0	2nd/3rd
70-90	4.8	2nd/3rd
80-100	5.6	3rd

STEERING

Type Rack and pinion, power assisted
Turns lock to lock 3.3

CONTROLS IN DETAIL

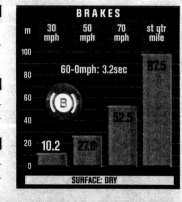

1 BMW air con controls don't do the rest of the cabin any justice aesthetically 2 Extra gauges distinguish Arnage's sporting pedigree 3 Five-speed ZF auto works much better than old GM four-speed item 4 Chrome eyeball vent one of only three carryover parts 5 Switchable traction control is standard 6 Leather wheel takes 20 hours to finish

SUSPENSION

Front Double wishbones with adaptive hydraulic damping
Rear Double wishbones with adaptive hydraulic damping

WHEELS & TYRES

Wheel size 7.5Jx17in
Made of Cast alloy
Tyres 255/55 WR17 Avon Turbospeed

BRAKES

Front 334mm ventilated discs
Rear 328mm ventilated discs
Anti-lock Standard

BRAKES

m	30 mph	50 mph	70 mph	st qtr mile
	10.2	27.0	52.5	87.5

60-0mph: 3.2sec
SURFACE: DRY

GEARING

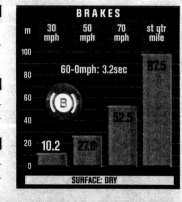

FUEL CONSUMPTION

TEST RESULTS

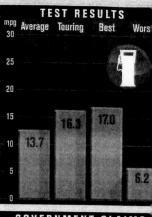

mpg	Average	Touring	Best	Worst
	13.7	16.3	17.0	6.2

GOVERNMENT CLAIMS

mpg	Urban	Extra urban	Combined
	12.0	21.5	16.7

Tank capacity: 94 litres (20.7 gallons)
Touring range: 350 miles

NOISE

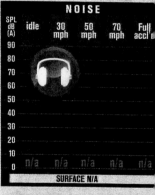

SPL dB (A)	idle	30 mph	50 mph	70 mph	Full accl
	n/a	n/a	n/a	n/a	n/a

SURFACE N/A

LAYOUT

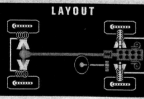

Body 4dr saloon **Front/rear tracks** 1608/1608mm **Turning circle** 12.4m **Min/max front leg room** 920/1070mm **Min/max rear leg room** 780/940mm
Min/max front head room 820/870mm **Rear head room** 875/885mm **Interior width front/rear** 1570/1570mm **Min/max boot width** 1100/1370mm
Boot length 830mm **Boot height** 460mm **VDA boot volume** 374 litres/dm³ **Kerb weight** 2330kg **Weight distribution f/r** 51/49 per cent **Max payload** 450kg

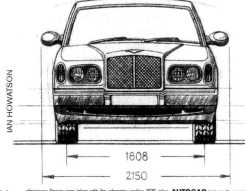

IAN HOWATSON

1608
2150

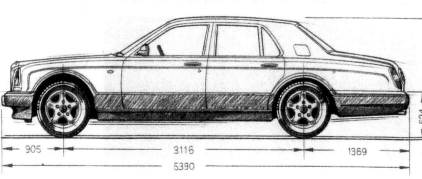

905   3116   1369
5390

1515
624

Performance figures were taken with the odometer reading 2932 miles. **AUTOCAR** test results are protected by world copyright and may not be reproduced without the editor's written permission

Although Bentley did admit that this car had had a hard life ... ectly prior to our test. There are no such complaints ... out the excellent drivetrain. ... e ZF gearbox has two modes: ... rmal and sport. In the latter, ... ultra-fast kickdown drops ... o gears with tremendous ... sto when the accelerator ... floored. It does so in one ... ooth action without a hint of ... atch from the transmission. A muted growl turns into a ... ll-blown roar as the revs rise ... yond 4000rpm during hard

The biggest letdown is the high level of wind noise generated on the motorway. A little road noise resonates through the cabin as well, but it is wind rustling around the A-pillars that provides the most aural discomfort.

A drag coefficient of 0.37 is fairly respectable for a car of such bulk, but it doesn't prevent the Bentley from having a healthy thirst for unleaded. Bentley claims the Arnage is 13.5 per cent more fuel efficient than the Turbo

Cabin is beautifully finished; seats are endlessly comfortable, supportive

Less room in rear seats than of old

...entley is more popular marque than RR right now. Boot is suitably vast

...cceleration. Momentum builds ... a fierce pace as each turbo ... elivers its maximum boost ... ressure of 0.7 bar. Although ... e RT's instant torque isn't ... eplicated wholly, throttle ... esponse is pleasingly crisp and ... urbo lag is all but eliminated. ...he Arnage's power delivery is ... uch more characterful than ... hat of the Seraph, but it's still ... ltra-refined at cruising speeds.

RT, but during our test we recorded a much smaller improvement. Overall, the 4398cc V8 drank a gallon of petrol every 13.7 miles (RT 13.3mpg). Over our touring route, during admittedly busier road conditions than normal, it managed 17.0mpg, just 0.5mpg less thirsty than the old car. And to fill the huge 94-litre tank you'll need at least £65 in

your back pocket. It'll last for 350 miles if you're careful.

If you're less precious about the fuel bills, you'll discover that the Arnage rides and handles like no Bentley before. The double wishbones front and rear are controlled by an adaptive damping system. It's capable of responding to the road conditions below each wheel in 0.01sec. The Arnage has stiffer suspension settings than the Seraph and is sharper on the road as a result. Make no mistake, the Bentley is still a huge machine to hustle, but it remains composed during hard cornering and has good body control considering there is so much of it. The one area where it loses out is in town, where the low-speed ride is a tad lumpy over broken surfaces.

This aside, the Arnage tolerates – even relishes – hard driving remarkably well. It steers with a good degree of accuracy and the helm weights up nicely as cornering forces rise. The body is 65 per cent stiffer than that of its predecessor

and there's a pleasing absence of creaks. This is not to say that Bentley has pulled off a miracle: a BMW 750i would still murder it along a country road. But it is a creditable effort and one that drivers of the Turbo RT should enjoy.

The fact that an Arnage costs £10,000 less than a Seraph is even better news. However, we find it difficult to accept that £145,000 does not buy bespoke switchgear. Like the Seraph, the Arnage uses BMW air con controls – disappointing in the context of the rest of the car.

The purchase of a Rolls-Royce or Bentley has never been a decision that could be described as rational. Buying an Arnage is an extravagance. It's the only way to justify having one when you consider that a pair of Mercedes S500s could be yours for £140,000. But neither would be a car from Crewe. And the fact is, this Arnage is the best Bentley saloon yet created. If ever there was a good reason to buy a Bentley, this is it.

WHAT IT COSTS

On-road price	£145,000
Total as tested	£145,000
Cost per mile	n/a

EQUIPMENT
(**bold** = options fitted to test car)

Automatic transmission	●
Cruise control	●
Anti-lock brakes	●
Airbag driver/passenger	●/●
CD player	●
Satellite navigation	£4700
Rear TV/video	£5895
Sunroof	£1200
Refrigerated compartment	£3800

● standard - not available

INSURANCE

Group	20
Typical quote	£1340

WARRANTY
3 years/unlimited miles, 8 years anti-corrosion, 3 years free recovery

SERVICING

Interim 10,000 miles/12 months	
Major 20,000 miles	
Max service cost £2800 (est)	

Objectively, Arnage is no match for cheaper S-class. Subjectively it's the other way round

...the most competent Bentley in hist...

The small print © Autocar 1998. Further information on the Bentley Arnage is available from Rolls-Royce Motor Cars Ltd, Crewe, Cheshire CW1 3PL (tel 01270 255155). The cost per mile figure is ...alculated over three years/36,000 miles and includes depreciation, maintenance, road tax, funding and fuel, but not insurance. The figure is supplied by Fleet Management Services (tel 01743 241121).

Bentley Azure

For Massive presence, beautiful cabin, amazing performance
Against A tad expensive, a tad thirsty, a tad old-fashioned

QUICK FACTS

Model tested	Azure
Price	£222,500
On sale	Now
0-60mph	5.9sec
Top speed	163mph
70-0mph	53.8m
Skidpan	0.85*g*
Economy	13.4mpg
CO2 emissions	495g/km

It would be terribly easy to take one look at the Bentley Azure, especially at its eye-watering list price of £222,500, and dismiss it as an anathema, an irrelevant dinosaur that no longer deserves a place on our roads in 2006. And neither Bentley nor the sort of customers for whom the all-new Azure has been created would care one iota if that's how the rest of the world received this car.

But for the small and exquisitely wealthy section of society that can afford a machine like the Azure there is, in fact, nothing else quite like it. Not, that is, until Rolls-Royce removes the lid from its Phantom to produce the new Corniche, due early next year (see page 49).

So what exactly is the Azure? And considering that Bentley's market research suggests potential buyers of this car will already own between five and 12 other cars, why would someone like that be remotely interested in owning it anyway?

The Azure was once a four-seat convertible version of the ancient Mulsanne Turbo – namely a huge, wobbly behemoth of a car with all the refinement of a small lorry, but featuring a delightfully antiquated interior and... that was about it.

The latest Azure really is new. Beneath its redesigned exterior (designed by Bentley design chief Dirk van Braeckel, who was also responsible for the Continental GT and the rag-top GTC), it's unrecognisable from the wheels up next to its predecessor. Bentley claims that, as a result, it's much sharper than the old Azure in every dimension.

Essentially, the Azure is an open version of the far newer Arnage T, but with a raft of modifications to make it as torsionally stiff as possible once the roof has been removed. The tweaks include carbonfibre cross-bracing and new front and rear subframes. The resulting bodyshell, says Bentley, is four times stiffer than before and, says *Autocar*, more graceful to look at compared with its ungainly predecessor.

Despite its many improvements, however, the Azure still uses an updated version of the 6.75-litre V8 that has been in service at Bentley (and Rolls-Royce, when the two companies were still related) since the beginning of time. Not that there's a great deal wrong with an engine that produces 450bhp at 4100rpm and (deep breath) 645lb ft at 3250rpm. That's almost 200lb ft more torque than a McLaren F1, in other words.

Trouble is, unlike the McLaren, the Azure uses a rather antiquated four-speed GM automatic gearbox to deploy its titanic forces and the engine itself is as heavy as it is handsome. The total kerb weight of this car is 2697kg, or, to put it another way, very nearly three Renaultsport Clio 197s. Which means the Azure needs all the torque it can muster if it's to provide the sort of performance Bentley – and its customers – require.

But, amazingly, perform it does. Bentley claims the Azure will do 168mph flat out. At our test track we ran out of steam (and bottle) at 163mph on the high-speed banking. At that point the Azure was pulling a highly impressive (and somewhat alarming) 1.05*g* of lateral cornering force. On the flat we've no doubt it would match Bentley's claim.

On the way to that speed, the Azure provides a vaguely surreal blend of refinement and raw acceleration, not to mention a range of noises from its engine that are nothing if not unique in 2006. Nothing can prepare you for what it feels like when you squeeze the →

New Azure's structure is far stiffer than old car's, giving sharper handling

BENTLEY AZURE DATA

WHAT IT COSTS

On-the-road price	£222,500
Price as tested	£222,500
Retained value 3yrs	na
Typical PCP pcm	na
Contract hire pcm	na
Cost per mile	na
CO₂	495g/km
Tax at 22/40% pcm	na/na
Insurance/typical quote	20/POA

EQUIPMENT CHECK LIST

Full leather interior ■
Satellite navigation ■
Four zone climate control ■
Parking sensors ■
Boot mounted 6CD changer ■

■ = Standard   na = not available

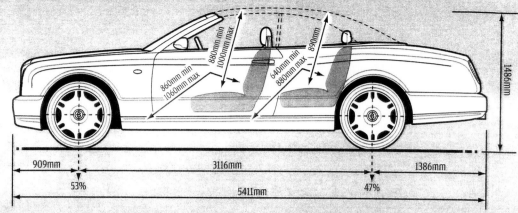

Front track 1610mm Rear track 1610mm Width including mirrors 1908m
Front interior width 1480mm Rear interior width 1530mm Boot space 310 litres

860mm min / 1060mm max
880mm min / 1000mm max
640mm min / 880mm max
890mm
1486mm
909mm   3116mm   1386mm
53%   5411mm   47%

SPECIFICATIONS

ENGINE

Type	8 cyls in vee, 6761cc
Made of	Alloy head and block
Installation	Front, longitudinal, rwd
Power	450bhp at 4100rpm
Torque	645lb ft at 3250rpm
Red line	4500rpm
Power to weight	167bhp per tonne
Torque to weight	239lb ft per tonne
Specific output	67bhp per litre
Bore/stroke	104.0/99.0mm
Compression ratio	7.8:1
Valve gear	2 per cyl, pushrods
Fuel type	Petrol

CHASSIS & BODY

Construction	Steel unibody
Weight	2695kg
Weight as tested	2710kg
Drag coefficient	0.33Cd
Wheels	8.0J x 19in
Made of	Alloy
Tyres	255/45 R19
	Pirelli P Zero
Spare	Foam kit

TRANSMISSION

Type	Rear-wheel drive
Gearbox	4-speed automatic
Ratios/mph per 1000rpm	
1st 2.48/11.5	2nd 1.48/19.3
3rd 1.00/28.5	4th 0.75/38.0
Final drive ratio	2.92:1

SUSPENSION

Front and rear Double wishbones, coil springs, electronic dampers, anti-roll bar

STEERING

Type	Hydraulic assistance, rack and pinion
Turns lock-to-lock	3.18
Turning circle	12.5m

To read our TOP 100 ROAD TESTS go to autocar.co.uk

BRAKES

Front	348mm ventilated discs
Rear	345mm ventilated discs
Anti-lock	Standard, with EBD and brake assist
Parking brake	Foot-operated

SAFETY

ESP electronic stability program. Driver, passenger and side airbags. Pop-up rollover bolsters

ROAD TEST RESULTS Dry, light breeze, 13C. Odometer reading 7750 miles

ACCELERATION
Standing qtr mile 14.3sec/100.7mph Standing km 25.7sec/132.0mph 30-70mph 5.1sec

mph	30	40	50	60	70	80	90	100	110	120	130	140
sec		2.4	3.3	4.5	5.9	7.5	9.3	11.6	14.2	17.1	20.8	25.4	30.3

BRAKING 60-0mph 3.19sec   Indicated mph at 30/70 30/71mph

	30mph-0	50mph-0	70mph-0
	9.3m	26.5m	53.8m

ACCELERATION IN GEAR

	Kickdown
20-40	1.8
30-50	2.1
40-60	2.6
50-70	3.0
60-80	3.4
70-90	4.1
80-100	4.8
90-110	5.4
100-120	6.6
110-130	8.3
120-140	9.5

MAX SPEEDS IN GEAR

AUTO
1) 52mph 4500 rpm
2) 87mph 4500 rpm
3) 128mph 4500 rpm
4) 163mph 4300 rpm

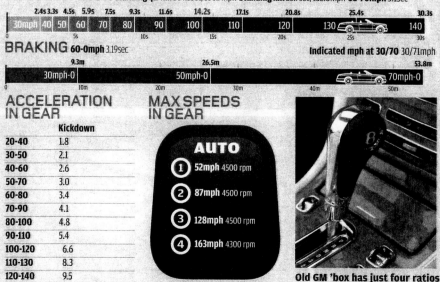

Old GM 'box has just four ratios

HANDLING

Lateral acceleration	0.85g
Balance	Understeer
Seat support	Poor

ECONOMY

TEST	Average	13.4mpg
	Touring	17.1mpg
	Track	5.3mpg
CLAIMED	Urban	9.2mpg
	Extra-urban	19.1mpg
	Combined	13.7mpg

Tank size 96 litres   **Test range** 321 miles

CABIN NOISE

Idle 40dBA **Max acceleration** 73dBA
30mph 61dBA **50mph** 65dBA **70mph** 69dBA

HEADLIGHTS

Dipped beam Good
Full beam Very good
Test notes. Fine range and power when dipped; very bright on full beam

PETER LIDDIARD

...ptuous cabin makes it easy to forgive below-par sat-nav and poor wipers

...ce is plentiful in front and back

Updated V8 packs almighty punch

ROLLS-ROYCE CORNICHE
The Azure's only rival – when it arrives

RIGHT NOW, the Bentley Azure has no direct competition; there are no other super-luxury four-seat convertibles on the market. But ex-Bentley partner Rolls-Royce is about to change all that with its second model: the Corniche.

Due in January, it will probably cost more than the Azure – the projected price is £250,000 – and will easily have as much (if not more) cachet. The Spirit of Ecstasy is a strong draw for those with as much money to spend on a car as most of us would borrow for a house.

Based on a shortened version of the Phantom's complex spaceframe, the Corniche uses that car's transmission and V12 engine, along with its interior. It's very similar to the 100EX concept

Rolls showed at the 2004 Geneva motor show, save for the interior, some of the detailing and the V16 engine.

It will inevitably weigh more than the Phantom's 2.5 tonnes, due to the extra bracing needed to make up for the lack of a roof, which may blunt performance slightly. Not that the 453bhp V12 is short of urge; it propels the Phantom to 60mph in 4.9sec, so the Corniche will be at least as quick as the Azure.

'The 453bhp Corniche will be at least as quick as the Azure'

New Corniche will be closely related to this 100EX convertible concept

...eliberately heavy accelerator all way to the thickly carpeted floor [ ] hold it there for a few seconds. [N]ot much happens to begin with, [ ] after perhaps half a second [ ] Azure [ ]mmons [ ]lf and, on [ ]uge wave [ ]orque, [ ]ply fires [ ]lf towards [ ]horizon [ ]h an [ ]uction [ ]se like a [ ]nt Hoover. [ ]n isolation [ ]numbers don't make especially [ ]eat reading: 0-30mph in 2.4sec, [ ]0mph in 5.9sec, 0-100mph in [ ]2sec and the standing quarter [ ]e in 14.3sec, with a terminal [ ]ed of 100.7mph. About the same [ ]a £20k Astra VXR, in other [ ]rds. But that's hardly the point. [I]n any case, the majestic way [ ]which the Azure summons its [ ]nsiderable thrust rarely leaves [ ]u wanting more. All in all, it [ ]rforms better than you could [ ]ssibly imagine, given its size and [ ]ight. Even its ancient four-speed [ ]arbox has been fettled to produce

Most Azure owners won't be doing this

smoothish upshifts and reasonably effective downshifts should, heaven forbid, you decide to stir the lever manually on the way into a corner. The inevitable penalty is an insatiable appetite for fuel. For the record, it did 5.3mpg at the track and averaged 13.4mpg.

The Azure is not in any way the sort of car you'd want to throw down the road – it's way too heavy for that – but if you drive it at seven-tenths it does most things extremely well, thanks to its reasonably accurate steering, taut body control and extraordinarily well resolved high-speed damping. It also stops well enough on the road, as long as you're prepared to give the pedal a good, hard shove, though at our test track it did suffer from considerable fade after only a couple of high-speed stops.

As for the ride, it's probably a little firmer than customers might expect at low speeds, but beneath

the sheen of vaguely sporting intent the Azure is actually a beautifully refined, comfortable car. Hood up, it generates more noise from its big Pirelli P-Zero tyres than is created by the wind at, say, 70mph. With the hood lowered, it is the most special place to be on four wheels – no more, no less – and that includes the rear bench seat, which feels like something out of _The Great Gatsby_.

Room is not an issue in the front or the rear (there is plenty in every direction), although boot space isn't quite as cavernous as you'd expect. For that, you can blame the

machinations of the all-electric hood, which eat into what would otherwise be an enormous boot.

Up front, the Azure is everything you'd expect of the world's most exclusive convertible, and then some. Yes, the wipers are from another era, the sat-nav isn't a patch on that of a humble Golf, and one or two of the details (such as the plastic handbrake release) are a bit cheap, but such is the level of appeal elsewhere that such things somehow don't matter. If ever a car could justify its price with its interior, the Azure is it.

AUTOCAR VERDICT

To most people, a car as heavy, thirsty and expensive as the Azure will seem completely pointless. Yet to the sort of customers for whom the Azure has been redesigned, none of this will matter. One thing's for sure, though: the world would be a lot less wonderful without cars like this on our roads.

The world's most exclusive convertible. And we like it, warts and all ★★★☆☆

Bentley Flying Spur

Bentleys are all about indomitable power and the sense of occasion. The Flying Spur has both in spades, but has it got the abilities to match its considerable appeal?

QUICK FACTS

Model tested	Flying Spur
Price	£115,000
On sale	Now
0-60mph	5.0sec
Top speed	202mph
70-0mph	49.2m
Skidpan	0.92g

t's the start of just another working day as you pass through the front door of your stately manor and crunch the gravel underfoot. In front of you sits your Bentley Continental Flying Spur, and as you clasp the weighty key – thankfully far removed from the VW item of the Continental GT – you can't help but feel a twinge of pride and satisfaction: you bought that. You've come a long way, achieved much in your life. You're a success. The Mercedes S-class you owned before the Spur never made you feel like that. There are a hundred expensive Mercedes in this affluent area, but only a handful of Bentleys.

If you understand only one thing about the Flying Spur, appreciate only one of its talents, it is this in-built marque appeal and gravitas that its rivals can only dream of. As we shall see, at times that's just as well.

The Flying Spur is the second stage of the rebirth of Bentley under parent company Volkswagen. It uses the same basic underpinnings as its more sporting GT coupé brother, albeit with considerable development under project leader Ulrich Eichhorn – of Ford Focus Mk1 and VW Golf Mk5 fame. That means air-sprung suspension and a lengthened steel chassis with 300mm added to the wheelbase, a twin-turbo W12 powerhouse up front with modifications to the exhaust, and the same wood-and-leather feast inside. Of course, there are also two extra doors and a lot more room behind the front seats. Both projects were actually started at the same time, but the Spur's development was put on ice while the GT was signed off and put into production.

STEPPING INSIDE

Back to the driveway. If the first reaction to seeing your Flying Spur was pride, we suspect your second reaction would be one of mild disappointment. During our time with the car, the styling won few friends and on the road it failed to gather the attention such a car should. It looks best when viewed either from the front or the rear, when traditional Bentley styling cues such as the mesh grille and heavily tapered rear create plenty of impact. Walk around to the side, however, and the general proportions – short bonnet, high roof, gently rounded corners – don't support the extravagant detailing and the bland, slab sides look especially clumsy. Beauty may be in the eye of the beholder, but a car such as this needs to make a confident statement, and in our opinion the Flying Spur doesn't.

Never mind. Open the large, weighty wood-and-leather wrapped door and settle into the driver's seat and all is nearly forgiven. The expanse of wood and leather – there's so much hide that you might feel guilty at the number of cows that have given their skin for your benefit – creates an interior with an emotional reach far beyond that of its German rivals. Wood, leather, chrome and old-English charm might not be the latest in design sophistication, but when they are combined to this standard few alternatives can match the sense of occasion.

Look closer and you'll notice the profusion of switches and knobs, and feel the rather hard, brittle black plastic from which most of the buttons are made – this feels like VW parts-bin engineering, and Audi does it much better. But you can't fault the overall effect, which is to make you feel as if you're sitting in the flight deck of an early jet aircraft.

In fact, where you really want to be is in the back, in one of the →

RANGE AT A GLANCE

PETROL		
Flying Spur	552bhp	£115,000
TRANSMISSION		
6-speed automatic, manual override		

DK05 CE

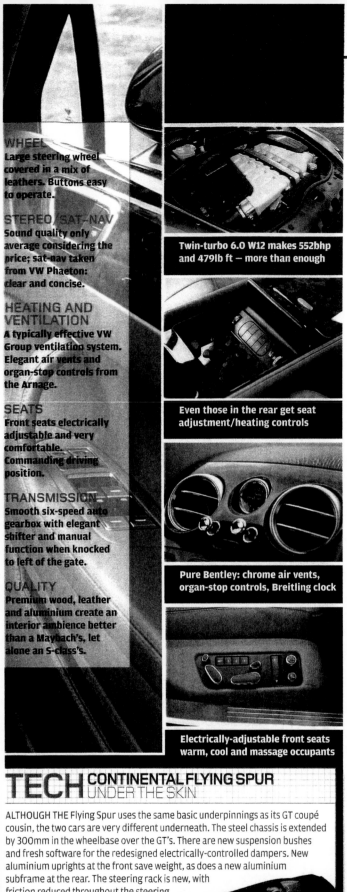

WHEEL
Large steering wheel covered in a mix of leathers. Buttons easy to operate.

STEREO / SAT-NAV
Sound quality only average considering the price; sat-nav taken from VW Phaeton: clear and concise.

HEATING AND VENTILATION
A typically effective VW Group ventilation system. Elegant air vents and organ-stop controls from the Arnage.

SEATS
Front seats electrically adjustable and very comfortable. Commanding driving position.

TRANSMISSION
Smooth six-speed auto gearbox with elegant shifter and manual function when knocked to left of the gate.

QUALITY
Premium wood, leather and aluminium create an interior ambience better than a Maybach's, let alone an S-class's.

Twin-turbo 6.0 W12 makes 552bhp and 479lb ft — more than enough

Even those in the rear get seat adjustment/heating controls

Pure Bentley: chrome air vents, organ-stop controls, Breitling clock

Electrically-adjustable front seats warm, cool and massage occupants

TECH
CONTINENTAL FLYING SPUR
UNDER THE SKIN

ALTHOUGH THE Flying Spur uses the same basic underpinnings as its GT coupé cousin, the two cars are very different underneath. The steel chassis is extended by 300mm in the wheelbase over the GT's. There are new suspension bushes and fresh software for the redesigned electrically-controlled dampers. New aluminium uprights at the front save weight, as does a new aluminium subframe at the rear. The steering rack is new, with friction reduced throughout the steering system. The W12 all-alloy engine is carried over from the GT, but the Flying Spur's exhaust has been redesigned for added refinement. Finally, the ZF automatic gearbox has been recalibrated to make more use of the engine's 479lb ft of torque.

Chassis, suspension, 'box all changed

← sumptuous rear chairs. Our test car had the £4510 twin seat option, upping the opulence even more. The two rear seats are separated by a long strip of wood veneer that houses individual climate control dials, heating and cooling controls for the seats themselves, and buttons for the electric adjustment of the backrest and of the base squab. There is a fantastic sense of space and luxury back here, especially when the front passenger seat is moved forward, as the nearside rear passenger has the power to do so from their control panel.

STARTING THE ENGINE
Back up front it's time to get going, so you turn the key in the barrel and wait for the starter motor to engage. There's a quick whirr before the W12 catches with a bassy whoomph and settles down to idle. What a mighty noise: rich, deep, classy and carrying

WHAT IT COSTS

BENTLEY CONTINENTAL FLYING SPUR

On-the-road price	£115,000	
Price as tested	£120,330	
Retained value 3yrs	na	
Typical PCP pcm	na	
Contract hire pcm	na	
Cost per mile	na	
CO_2	423g/km	
Tax at 22/40% pcm	£772/£1403	
Insurance/typical quote	20/£809	

EQUIPMENT CHECK LIST

Electric s/wheel adjust	■	
Dual-zone climate control	■	
Auto headlights/wipers	■	
Xenon headlights	■	
Cruise control	■	
Electric windows front/rear	■	
Airbags front/side/curtain	■	
Emergency brake assist	■	
ESP/traction control	■	
Rear ISOFIX seat mountings	na	
Metallic paint	■	
Wheel upgrades, from	£1130	☛
Alloy fuel filler cap	£160	⚑
Leather seats	■	
Heated front seats	■	
Heated steering wheel	£310	⚑
Veneer upgrade	£950	⚑
Keyless go	na	
CD multichanger	■	
TV Receiver	**£820**	⚑
Satellite navigation	■	
Parking sensors	■	
Electric solar sunroof	£620	☛
Bluetooth connection	£390	⚑
Tyre pressure sensors	■	
Split/folding rear seats	na	
Four-seat interior	**£4510**	⚑

Options in **bold** fitted to test car
*denotes option as part of a package
■ = Standard na = not available
⚑ Buy it ☛ Consider it ⚑ Forget it

the same promise of titanic torque you might sense standing next to the Flying Scotsman. The Spur responds immediately to a prod of the throttle: a blip at standstill rocks the structure, and acceleration from rest has the sort of commanding authority only cars like this seem to muster. With 5998cc, twin turbochargers and twin intercoolers boosting the unusual 'W' configuration – effectively two narrow-angle V6 engines spliced on a common crankshaft – the Spur isn't deficient in the engine room. Due to the work carried out on the exhaust, the Spur is noticeably quieter and less bassy than the GT.

Before we actually consider the Bentley's performance, let's make clear the task that faces the W12. This is a car that weighs 2515kg with fuel but without occupants: a two-and-a-half-tonne mass of metal, wood and leather. And here's the amazing bit: it will fly from 0-60mph in 5.0sec, 100mph in 12.8sec and 140mph in 27.7sec. And then, as we recently discovered at the Nardo track in Italy, it can go on to 202mph.

From behind the large, flat steering wheel, accessing this mighty performance is surreal: simply squeeze the right pedal and feel the force. At low speeds it glides forward with only a subtle but audible murmur: it's clear that Bentley wasn't aiming for noiseless refinement, instead opting for a hint of sporting intent. Accelerate hard and the W12 growls with a note just on the pleasing side of coarse, the six-speed automatic gearbox changing ratios quickly and fluently. The new programming in the ZF gearbox relies more on the engine's torque than in the GT, which suits the car's character well. You can also change gears manually with either the gearstick in tiptronic mode or the rather cheap-feeling plastic paddles behind the steering wheel.

Once you've held the throttle pedal to the carpet for a while, the Spur's performance really hits home. This is a car that only really starts to feel truly quick above 100mph, when the way the speedometer needle stealthily flies past the 130, 140, 150 and 160mph markings is extraordinary. Stability is excellent at speed – the product of the aerodynamic work Bentley has done to allow the Spur to handle such high speeds with ease.

ON THE ROAD
So it's quick, then, but how does it ride? The adjustable damping is accessed by a small button in a row of many behind the gearlever, and altered by turning the main control wheel in the centre of the dashboard. There are five settings between the extremes of comfort → turn to p40

BENTLEY FLYING SPUR DATA

ESTERS' NOTES

he field of vision from the
earside door mirror verges on
he useless. In such a big car,
manoeuvre means a
ightening series of nervous
ances over your shoulder.

he Spur really feels in a niche
its own: it combines the
seability of a Mercedes
class with the sense of
ccasion of an Arnage. This car
n't white goods – it's a very
ecial way to travel.

Front track 1623mm **Rear track** 1607mm **Width including mirrors** 2118mm
Front interior width 1490mm

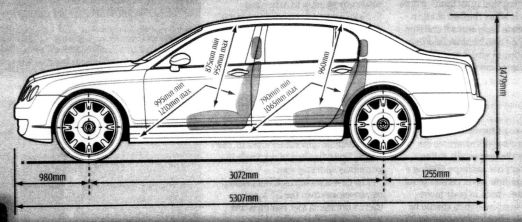

980mm 3072mm 1255mm
5307mm

SPECIFICATIONS

ENGINE

Type	W12, 5998cc, twin turbos
Made of	Alloy head and block
Installation	Front, longitudinal, 4wd
Power	552bhp at 6100rpm
Torque	479lb ft at 1600 rpm
Red line	6300rpm
Power to weight	223bhp per tonne
Torque to weight	193lb ft per tonne
Specific output	92bhp per litre
Bore/stroke	84.0/90.2mm
Compression ratio	9.0:1
Valve gear	4 per cyl, dohc
Management	Bosch
Fuel type	Petrol

CHASSIS & BODY

Construction	Steel unibody
Weight	2475kg
Weight as tested	2515kg
Drag coefficient	0.31
Wheels	9.0J x 19in
Made of	Alloy
Tyres	275/40 R19
	Pirelli
Spare	None (repair kit)

TRANSMISSION

Type	Four-wheel drive
Gearbox	6-speed automatic
Ratios/mph per 1000rpm	
1st 4.17/5.4 **2nd** 2.34/9.7 **3rd** 1.52/14.9	
4th 1.14/19.9 **5th** 0.87/26.1 **6th** 0.69/32.9	
Final-drive ratio	3.52

SUSPENSION

Front Four-link, air springs	
Rear Multi-link, air springs	

STEERING

Type Speed-sensitive power-assisted rack and pinion	
Turns lock-to-lock	2.8
Turning circle	11.8m

BRAKES

Front 405mm ventilated discs	
Rear 335mm ventilated discs	
Anti-lock Standard	
Parking brake Electric	

SAFETY

Driver, passenger, curtain and front and rear side
airbags, seatbelt pre-tensioners, traction control, ESP

ROAD TEST RESULTS Dry weather, minimal wind, 20 degrees

ACCELERATION **Standing qtr mile** 13.8sec/103.6mph **Standing km** 24.9sec/134.1mph **30-70mph** 4.9sec

2.0s	3.0s	3.9s	5.0s	6.8s	8.6s	10.2s	12.8s	15.7s	18.6s	22.9s	27.6s
30mph	40	50	60	70	80	90	100	110	120	130	140

BRAKING **60-0mph** 3.0sec

Indicated mph at 30/70 31/73mph

9.1m 25.1m 49.2m
30mph-0 50mph-0 70mph-0

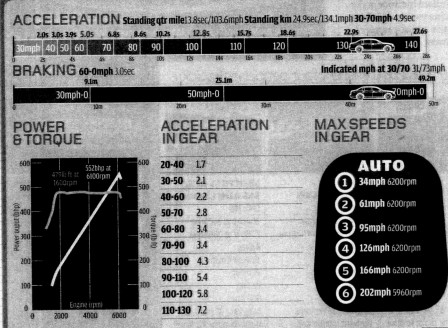

POWER & TORQUE

479lb ft at 1600rpm
552bhp at 6100rpm

ACCELERATION IN GEAR

20-40	1.7
30-50	2.1
40-60	2.2
50-70	2.8
60-80	3.4
70-90	3.4
80-100	4.3
90-110	5.4
100-120	5.8
110-130	7.2

MAX SPEEDS IN GEAR

AUTO

①	34mph	6200rpm
②	61mph	6200rpm
③	95mph	6200rpm
④	126mph	6200rpm
⑤	166mph	6200rpm
⑥	202mph	5960rpm

HANDLING

Lateral acceleration	0.92g
Balance	understeer
Seat support	average

ECONOMY

TEST	**Average**	14.1mpg
	Touring	16.4mpg
	Track	5.1mpg
CLAIMED	**Urban**	21.6mpg
	Extra-urban	32.8mpg
	Combined	27.7mpg

Tank size 78 litres **Test range** 242 miles

CABIN NOISE

Idle 48dbA **Max revs in third gear** 73dbA
30mph 61dbA **50mph** 63dbA **70mph** 67dbA

HEADLIGHTS

Dipped beam Very good **Full beam** Excellent
Test notes Turn night into day

VERDICT & RIVALS p40→

from p37 ← and sport, the default being halfway between the two. It is in this setting that most Spurs will be driven, as it offers the best compromise between body control and ride comfort, and also because fiddling with the control wheel every time the road surface or environment changes quickly becomes a pain.

In this mode, the primary ride of the Spur over road undulations is very good, with a suitably aristocratic waftiness to its forward motion. The major disappointment is the secondary ride, especially at low speeds over poor surfaces. Hitting a sunken manhole cover creates more commotion – both in body movement and in noise – than should be expected in a luxury limousine such as this. And the great pity is that tuning the dampers for extra comfort only really makes the car wallow more – it doesn't allow it to contain road blemishes in a more cosseting way. Such obstacles send a muffled shimmer through the structure at times, too, as if the dampers are struggling to contain the situation.

There is also significant kickback through the steering wheel and too much noise filters into the cabin – from the rear suspension in particular – along with a surprising amount of wind noise at speed. This is a Bentley, and we fully appreciate it needs a sporting bias, but the Flying Spur is also a luxury limousine, and the ability to offer an absorbant ride has to be the primary objective. A long-wheelbase Jaguar XJ offers a much more settled ride, for considerably less money.

Still, you're behind the wheel, not in the back, and the long drive of your stately home leads directly onto a classic English B-road. You never made any attempt to drive your S-class in a sporting manner, but the Spur is different because, despite its size and weight, it is fun to hustle along at speed. Adjust the dampers to sport, accept the choppiness to the secondary ride and marvel at the way the Spur grips and changes direction. You can push harder in this car than you would think possible, and despite the early onset of tyre squeal when the inevitable understeer kicks in, the Flying Spur digs in and responds in a genuinely sporting way.

The new steering rack is a marked improvement over the GT's, too: there's not much feel, but then this isn't a Lotus Elise, and you can steer the Flying Spur with much greater accuracy and confidence than you can the GT – especially during turn-in.

The brakes deserve a special mention. Despite being regular metal items, they are the largest discs fitted to any production car on the front axle at 405mm. The result is supreme retardation considering the mass they have to slow – something you feel Bentley needed to make sure of considering the car's top speed. But their real talent is the ability to resist fade, despite several repeated full stops from high three-figure speeds. That Bentley has managed this is astonishing.

Driven hard like this, the Spur's thirst is truly frightening. But then this is a car that achieves 15mpg on a good day. Your wallet might be fat to enable you to afford the Spur in the first instance, but you're unlikely to be pleased with a realistic range of 200 miles between fill-ups.

Flying Spur a surprisingly able handler for such a leviathan

Width 1040mm

Depth 1265mm

Height 460mm

Boot is a good length, but relatively narrow and shallow: 475 litres just not big enough for the luxury class

INSTANT GROUP TEST Four ways to transport four people very quickly

COMFORT CHOICE

DRIVER'S CHOICE

Special doesn't begin to describe how the interior feels (and makes you feel); proof that leather and wood still have a place inside cars

Unsettled ride biggest dynamic failing, especially at low speeds; shame as Bentley has suitable waftiness over smooth surfaces

MAKE	BENTLEY Continental	ALPINA	AUDI	MERCEDES-BENZ
Model	Flying Spur	B7	A8 6.0 W12 LWB	S65 AMG Limousine
Price	£115,000	£83,850	£77,360	£142,740
Power	552bhp at 6100rpm	493bhp at 5500rpm	444bhp at 6200rpm	604bhp at 5100rpm
Torque	479lb ft at 1600rpm	516lb ft at 4250rpm	427lb ft at 4000-4700rpm	737lb ft at 2000rpm
0-60mph	5.0sec	5.1sec	5.2sec	4.4sec
Top Speed	202mph	186mph	155mph (limited)	155mph (limited)
Fuel consumption	14.1mpg (test figure)	18.2mpg	20.5mpg	19.0mpg
Kerbweight	2515kg	2000kg	1995kg	2220kg
Boot space	475 litres	500 litres	500 litres	500 litres
CO₂/Tax band	423g/km / 35 per cent	309g/km / 35 per cent	331g/km / 35 per cent	317g/km / 35 per cent
We think	Tremendous headline top speed and sense of occasion from big Bentley. Ride less composed than it should be.	The sporting choice to drive and mightily quick with it. A totally different experience to the Flying Spur.	Fantastic interior and a bargain in this company. But without the turbos the W12 isn't quite as impressive.	Mighty bi-turbo V12 makes the Bentley's engine seem anaemic. Can't match the Bentley's aura.
VERDICT	★★★☆☆	★★★☆☆	★★★☆☆	★★★★☆

TEST SCORECARD

ENGINE ★★★★☆
Monstrous thrust from characterful twin-turbo W12, with just the right amount of refinement for the purpose.

TRANSMISSION ★★★★☆
Very smooth-shifting six-speed auto 'box works surprisingly well with semi-automatic paddles. Occasional hesitancy at walking pace.

STEERING ★★★☆☆
Guides the Spur with reasonable precision. Suitably light at low speeds; confidence-inspiring at high ones. Too much kickback.

BRAKES ★★★★★
Fantastic stopping power, and barely believable resistance to fade in the circumstances.

HANDLING ★★★★☆
Considering the forces involved in containing the 2515kg kerbweight, rather good. Can be chucked about with enthusiasm – up to a point.

RIDE ★★★☆☆
Wafts along at speed with authority, but simply doesn't absorb poor road surfaces as it should. There's also too much road roar.

ECONOMY ★★☆☆☆
Huge thirst. More serious in this market is the restricted 200-mile range, despite 78-litre fuel tank.

DRIVING POSITION & VISIBILITY ★★★☆☆
Commanding driving position, but tiny and heavily magnified passenger door mirror creates a large blind spot.

INSTRUMENTS & CONTROLS ★★★★☆
Clear, expensive-looking instrumentation. The mass of switchgear won't be to everyone's tastes.

EQUIPMENT ★★★★☆
As you would expect at this price: comprehensive.

LIVEABILITY ★★★☆☆
If you discount parking it (it's 5.3m long) and fuelling it, living with the Spur should be easy.

QUALITY ★★★★☆
A real depth to the quality inside the attractive cabin: good materials, feels well put together.

VALUE ★★★☆☆
Costs more than mainstream rivals such as a Mercedes S600, but considerably cheaper than (more powerful) S65 AMG – Flying Spur is in a niche of its own. Residuals should be class-leading.

SAFETY ★★★★☆
Eight airbags, including two full-length curtain 'bags, ESP, four-wheel drive, anti-lock brakes and emergency brake assist.

AUTOCAR VERDICT
There is much to love about the Flying Spur: it creates a sense of occasion like few other cars and offers an endearing blend of performance and braking power. It's even fun to drive, in a brutish kind of way. However, the ride, refinement and overall appearance just aren't good enough. The Flying Spur is a flawed giant.

Feel-good but flawed super-limousine ★★★☆☆

Bentley Continental GT

o the latest revisions keep this grand tourer in the top league?

DDEL TESTED Continental GT

rice £135,760 ● **Power** 567bhp ● **Torque** 516lb ft ● **0-60mph** 4.6sec
uel economy 14.7mpg ● **CO₂ emissions** 384g/km ● **70-0mph** 44.7m ● **Skidpan** 1.05g

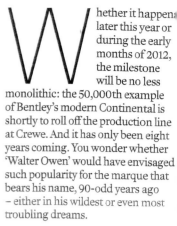

hether it happens later this year or during the early months of 2012, the milestone will be no less monolithic: the 50,000th example of Bentley's modern Continental is shortly to roll off the production line at Crewe. And it has only been eight years coming. You wonder whether 'Walter Owen' would have envisaged such popularity for the marque that bears his name, 90-odd years ago – either in his wildest or even most troubling dreams.

E LIKE Extraordinary engine ● Capable handling ● Distance-shrinking ability

1 he body line out of the front wheel is reminiscent of pre-war ntleys, when the wing and lywork were separate. The rcedes CLS tries something ilar, but less successfully.

2 These are one of two 21in wheel options; 20s are standard. All are available polished, chromed or painted.

3 Seemingly, all manufacturers want 'jewelled'-effect headlights these days. The Continental GT's are prettier than most.

4 The complex-looking grille is a throwback to Bentleys of old. Looks great; proves a pain to clean. The grille is more upright than its predecessor's.

Either way, eight years after its debut, it's about time that the Continental GT coupé, bedrock of Bentley's current sales volume, had a mid-life facelift. This isn't an all-new car, although Crewe would like you to believe it is. The generously proportioned two-plus-two has been put on a diet, given a styling massage inside and out, and had some telling mechanical updates.

So with more power, less weight, a roomier cabin and a more sporting chassis, can this Bentley answer our requirements of a sports car and grand tourer better than the 2003 original?

DESIGN AND ENGINEERING

★★★★☆

The very latest aluminium superforming production technology has allowed Bentley's design team, lead by Dirk van Braeckel, much greater freedom for sculpture in the new Continental's panels, carved into which are sharper, more pronounced creases and curves than the original could ever have had. The updated GT looks contemporary and sacrifices a little of the original's simple elegance →

WE DON'T LIKE Poor fuel economy ● Interior layout failings ● Heavier than it ought to be

DKII CAV

5 **Oval exhaust pipes, reminiscent of the rear light shapes (a real novelty when this car was launched), are only finishers. The meat of the exhausts is circular.**

6 **Winged badge includes a 'B' that, with a push, is the button for the boot release.**

7 **Rear wing (visible in the rear-view mirror) pops up at speed to reduce lift at the rear and increase stability.**

8 **Is this the world's largest high-level brake light? It's wide enou to virtually be a design feature. It lights up across its entire width so there's little excuse for rear-endin Continental GT.**

1 The centrally mounted Breitling clock is subtle, relatively clear and extremely classy.

2 Bentley's traditional 'organ stop' air vent control levers remain, and they still feel great.

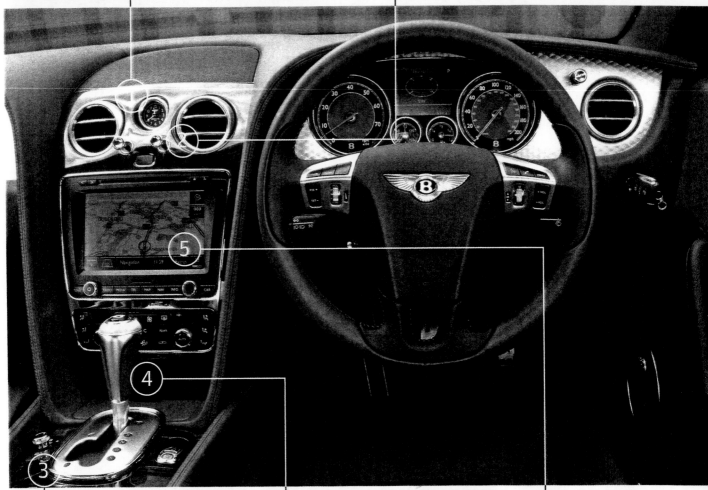

5

4

3

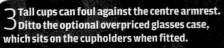

3 Tall cups can foul against the centre armrest. Ditto the optional overpriced glasses case, which sits on the cupholders when fitted.

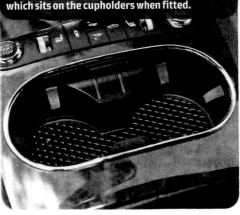

4 Gearlever is still unashamedly big and chunky, when we've become accustomed to subtle and electronic. Old school, but nicely finished.

5 The infotainment system is straight fro Volkswagen. Visually, it's a bit clunky compared with the best on offer elsewhere

Inside out

HOW BIG IS IT?

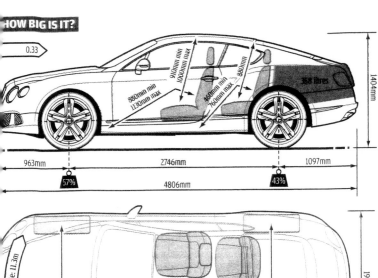

0.33

910mm min
1000mm max
880mm
460mm min
700mm max
880mm min
1130mm max
358 litres
1404mm

963mm — 2746mm — 1097mm
57% — 43%
4806mm

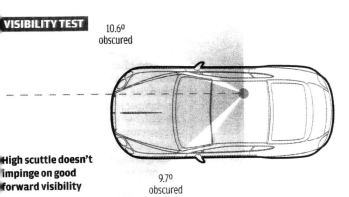

Turning circle: 11.3m
1664mm — 1655mm
1944mm

VISIBILITY TEST

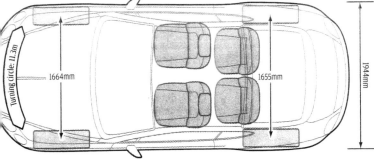

10.6º obscured

9.7º obscured

High scuttle doesn't impinge on good forward visibility

Front seats and steering wheel are new. Finish is first rate, ergonomics less

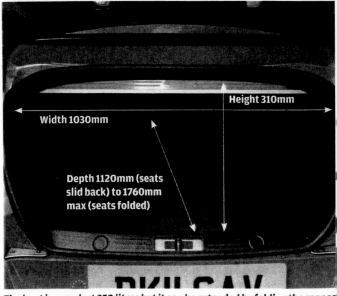

Thinner front seats give 46mm extra rear legroom but adults still feel cram

Height 310mm

Width 1030mm

Depth 1120mm (seats slid back) to 1760mm max (seats folded)

The boot is a modest 358 litres but it can be extended by folding the rear se

---

← for greater visual muscularity. To our eyes, it's an appealing compromise.

But the new styling is only quietly suggestive of what Bentley has done to the mechanicals of this car to make it a match for the Aston Martins, Ferraris and Porsches of this decade. The updated GT's body is 40mm wider than it was, and the track widths of its chassis are 41mm greater up front and 48mm greater at the rear.

The original GT's major chassis constituents are carried over. There are 'four-link' double wishbones up front and a multi-link arrangement at the rear, mounted on to the car's steel monocoque body via lightweight, high-strength cast aluminium uprights. Bentley has reappraised spring and damper rates on the GT's continuously controlled air suspension, however, and redesigned its front anti-roll bar. It's also offering 21in alloy wheels for the first time on a standard Continental GT.

Engine and drivetrain updates are many, too. Lighter, lower-friction internals in Bentley's forced-induction W12 engine work alongside new lower-inertia turbochargers and a new ECU to produce 567bhp from 5998cc. More enticing is the prospect of a 37lb ft gain in torque, up to 516lb ft.

That extra urge finds its way to the road through an updated ZF six-speed automatic gearbox, and via all four wheels, with torque juggled between front and rear axles by a Torsen torque-sensing centre differential that apportions a default 60 per cent of it to the rear axle in normal conditions.

Elsewhere, a 65kg saving has been made thanks to lightweight seats, among other things. Aerodynamic drag and aerodynamic lift have also been reduced – a measure that's of more import on a car capable of almost 200mph than on anything with a 155mph electronic speed limiter.

INTERIOR

★★★½☆

It would be entirely fair to record that Bentley hasn't 'reinvented the wheel' inside the revised Conti – if it weren't for the fact that a new steering wheel is actually chief among the revisions. The new tiller is smaller in diameter than before and acts on the front wheels via a slightly faster steering rack.

Most of the cabin is carried over from the superseded car, however – and for the most part, that's no bad thing at all. In our test car, soft →

rack notes

RY CIRCUIT

Bentley Continental GT
min 18.1sec
ston Martin
irage Volante
min 16.2sec

iven its weight, the
entley performs rather
dmirably around the dry
andling circuit, offering
ood grip and resistance
o overheating its tyres
nd brakes.

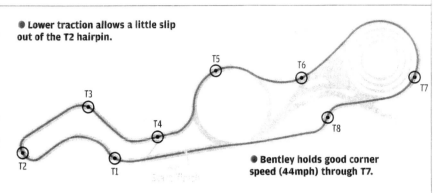

● **Stability is good through the high-speed T4 corner.**

● **GT has superb traction out of the tightest hairpin.**

ET CIRCUIT

entley Continental GT
min 15.4sec
ston Martin
irage Volante
min 15.1sec

ur wet handling circuit is
owing as its surface wears,
ut the Bentley made light
ork of it anyway. It's grippy
nd has lots of traction
verywhere.

● **Lower traction allows a little slip out of the T2 hairpin.**

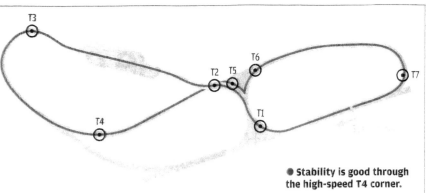

● **Bentley holds good corner speed (44mph) through T7.**

CCELERATION 18deg C, dry

ENTLEY CONTINENTAL GT

tanding quarter mile 13.1sec at 110.0mph, standing km 23.6sec at 141.9mph, 30-70mph 4.2sec, 30-70mph in fourth na

30	40	50	60	70	80	90	100	110	120mph	130mph	140mph	150mph
1.8s	2.8s	3.6	4.6	6.0s	7.5s	9.0s	10.9s	13.2s	15.6s	18.6s	22.9s	27.5s

STON MARTIN VIRAGE VOLANTE

tanding quarter mile 13.5sec at 110.6mph, standing km 23.8sec at 144.3mph, 30-70mph 4.2sec, 30-70mph in fourth 8.2sec

30	40	50	60	70	80	90	100	110	120mph	130mph	140mph	150mph
2.1s	3.0	4.0s	4.9	6.3s	7.7s	9.2s	10.9s	13.0s	15.3s	17.9s	21.8s	26.2s

RAKING 60-0mph 2.5sec

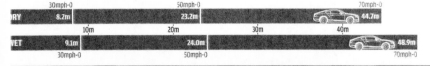

	30mph-0	50mph-0	70mph-0
RY	8.2m	23.2m	44.7m
ET	9.1m	24.0m	48.9m

n the limit

he advantage of the Bentley running on air springs
the flexibility to pick between varying degrees of
de quality and body control. Most of the time, we
ft them in a middling setting, but if you're pushing

on, there's reward in setting them more stiffly. Do so
and the Bentley shows impressive resistance to dive
under braking and, while you'd never call it agile on
turn-in, it hauls itself into corners with conviction.

The GT's steering weights up well, too — the force
generated by planting the best part of a tonne on an
outside front wheel at more than 1.0g translate
rather easily to giving road feel through the rim.

← embroidered leathers, attractive
walnut veneers, handmade aluminiu
fascia inserts and chrome-bezelled
control dials all contributed to a
superbly rich and luxurious 'old
English' cabin ambience that few
car makers can pull off. And the GT's
cabin is made all the more special by
Bentley's own touches of distinction,
such as its organ-stop air vent contro

Fit and finish in our test car was
excellent – as it should be from Crew
self-proclaimed 'master craftsmen',
whose attention to detail would still
seem to be the envy of the industry.

The biggest substantive difference
inside comes courtesy of two new,
slimmed-down, scalloped front seats
which, claims Bentley, liberate an ext
46mm of legroom for rear passenger
The extra space is welcome, but it
doesn't transform the GT into a car fi
for four adults. In the back, headroor
for anyone over six feet tall is still tigh

Up front, while the new touchscree
multimedia system is welcome,
there's still room for improvement
in some areas. The ergonomics of
the column stalks leaves a little to be
desired, too; you'll lose count of the
number of times you tug on the left-
hand gearchange paddle while you're
fumbling for the indicators. Equally
frustrating is the fact that changing
the damper settings from Comfort,
through two intermediate settings,
to Sport means pressing a button on
the transmission tunnel and then
cycling through a menu on the fascia-
mounted touchscreen.

PERFORMANCE

★★★★☆

Any car that weighs 2320kg yet can
still sprint to 60mph in 4.6sec and to
100 in 10.9sec is not exactly short of a
spot of shove.

The Continental GT's engine is
from the top division of internally

On its softer settings, the Conti delivers sufficient long-haul ride comfort

Under the skin

BIOFUEL MODIFICATIONS

Following on from the engine in the 2009 Continental Supersports coupé, Bentley's W12 engine for the new, Euro 5-compliant Continental GT can run on regular unleaded, E85 biofuel, or any mixture of the two.

A quality sensor in the fuel delivery system detects the blending ratio of the fuel being supplied. It then feeds data to the engine's ECU, which adapts the engine's fuelling and valve timing to ensure that power and torque remain consistent.

The engine's hardware had to be modified to handle the more corrosive properties of bioethanol. Two variable-flow fuel pumps and a closed loop fuel rail were fitted. Also, every O-ring, seal, gasket and pipe in the fuel system had to be re-specified, and new valve coating and valve seats fitted.

combusted performance, capable of delivering great gobs of urge at will. The key to the flexibility comes not when the engine is making 6000rpm and peak power, but when the big turbochargers begin to spool up. This exceptional powerplant makes its peak 516lb ft at just 1700rpm.

At pretty much any revs, in any gear, the Bentley is as flexible as you'd hope for a car whose primary purpose is to make countries feel smaller. Squirt the throttle at the start of a motorway sliproad at 30mph and 4.2sec later you'll be at 70mph. Do the same at 50mph and 70mph is just 2.4sec away.

Is it wrong, then, to hope for more than six forward speeds from the standard automatic gearbox? And for a more advanced-feeling shift than its clonk-through mechanical lever? Perhaps. Being able to just electronically select 'D' and then run the show from brilliantly placed column paddles adds an air of sophistication to an Aston Martin's or Ferrari's drivetrain that the Continental GT's ill-placed and plasticky-feeling paddles can't match.

But never did we want for more than the six speeds that the Bentley brings with it. Truth be told, a power unit this flexible would probably deliver admirable performance driving only on its even gears.

In its upper gears, the GT's performance is refined and leggy, but we suspect it could cope with an even longer top-gear stride, even to the other side of 40mph per 1000rpm, which would help its touring economy figure. As it is, even with a blown 6.0-litre engine, we'd hope to return a spot more than 22mpg during an undemanding cruise.

Conversely, there is nothing in the slightest bit disappointing about the Continental GT's optional carbon-ceramic brakes, supposing you can look past their price. Capable of hauling the GT from 60mph to rest in just 2.5sec in the dry (and 2.6sec in the wet), they have exceptional stopping power and resistance to fade.

RIDE AND HANDLING

★★★★☆

Included in our particular test car's comprehensive list of options are 21in alloy wheels shod with 275/35 ZR21 Pirelli P Zero tyres. These are not necessarily conducive to providing a ride that's appropriate for a cross-continental grand tourer, especially →

The W12 meets stricter Euro 5 emissions regs and can now run on E85 bio

Some 57 per cent of the Continental's weight is on the front end and this car runs on the same size tyres all round. Given also that the front wheels have to cope with steering forces and power distribution, it is almost inevitable that, when the Bentley runs out of grip, it does so from the front first.

With stability control switched on, this results in a subtle and quick intervention from the electronics.

With it switched off, the understeer will continue unless you give a judicious lift or trailing of the brakes, but regardless of provocation, this is not a car (wet aside) that will oversteer enthusiastically

Crunching numbers

ENGINE
Installation	Front, longitudinal
Type	W12, 5998cc, petrol
Made of	Aluminium block and head
Bore/stroke	90.2mm/84.0mm
Compression ratio	9.0:1
Valve gear	4 per cyl
Power	567bhp at 6000rpm
Torque	516lb ft at 1700-5400rpm
Red line	6250rpm
Power to weight	244bhp per tonne
Torque to weight	222lb ft per tonne
Specific output	95bhp per litre

POWER & TORQUE

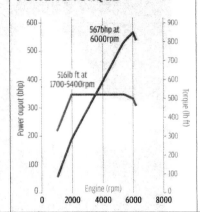

567bhp at 6000rpm
516lb ft at 1700-5400rpm

CHASSIS & BODY
Construction	Steel monocoque
Weight/as tested	2320kg/2375kg
Drag coefficient	0.33
Wheels	9.5Jx21in
Tyres	275/35 ZR21
Spare	Space saver (optional)

TRANSMISSION
Type	4-wheel drive
Gearbox	6-speed automatic
Ratios/mph per 1000rpm	
1st 4.17/5.8	**2nd** 2.34/10.3
3rd 1.52/15.9	**4th** 1.14/21.1
5th 0.87/27.7	**6th** .069/34.9
Final drive ratio	3.526

ECONOMY
TEST	Average	14.7mpg
	Touring	22.1mpg
	Track	7.0mpg
CLAIMED	Urban	11.1mpg
	Extra-urban	24.9mpg
	Combined	17.1mpg
	Tank size	90 litres
	Test range	291 miles

SUSPENSION
Front 'Four link' double wishbones, self-levelling air suspension, anti-roll bar
Rear Trapezoidal multi-link, self-levelling air suspension, anti-roll bar

STEERING
Type	Electro-hydraulic, rack and pinion
Turns lock to lock	2.6
Turning circle	11.3m

BRAKES
Front	420mm ventilated discs
Rear	356mm ventilated discs
Anti-lock	Standard, EBD, Brake Assist

CABIN NOISE
Idle 47dB	Max revs in third gear 76dB
30mph 57dB	50mph 63dB 70mph 66dB

SAFETY
ABS, Brake Assist, ESP
EuroNCAP crash rating Not tested

GREEN RATING
CO_2 emissions 384g/km
Tax at 20/40% pcm £786/£1572

ACCELERATION
MPH	TIME (sec)
0-30	1.8
0-40	2.8
0-50	3.6
0-60	4.6
0-70	6.0
0-80	7.5
0-90	9.0
0-100	10.9
0-110	13.2
0-120	15.6
0-130	18.6
0-140	22.9
0-150	27.5
0-160	-

ACCELERATION IN KICKDOWN
MPH	sec
20-40	1.0
30-50	1.8
40-60	1.8
50-70	2.4
60-80	2.9
70-90	3.0
80-100	3.5
90-110	4.2
100-120	4.7
110-130	5.4
120-140	7.3
130-150	9.0

MAX SPEEDS IN GEAR
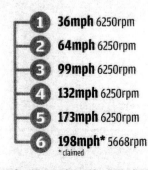

1. **36mph** 6250rpm
2. **64mph** 6250rpm
3. **99mph** 6250rpm
4. **132mph** 6250rpm
5. **173mph** 6250rpm
6. **198mph*** 5668rpm

* claimed

RPM in 6th @ 70/80mph = 2004/2290

DEPRECIATION
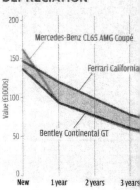

Mercedes-Benz CL65 AMG Coupé
Ferrari California
Bentley Continental GT

AUTOCAR ROAD TEST
Read all of our road tests autocar.co.uk

given the inconsistent ride quality of
is car's immediate predecessor.

It's true that the revised Continental
T does not smooth out surface
nperfections with the aplomb of,
ay, a Mercedes CL. But those who
ssume that it cannot ride have
ot considered the relative benefit
f two and-a-bit tonnes riding on
s springs. Persuading all of those
ilograms to offer anything other than
nmunity from surface imperfections
a feat in itself. It goes to making the
ontinental GT, particularly on its
ofter spring settings, a vastly capable
ng-distance cruiser. There is good
traight-line stability, too.

All of which comes at some kind of
rice. Aston Martins, fast Porsche 911s
nd the Maserati GranTurismo are, at
heir heart, sports cars that have been
ersuaded to become long-distance
rand touring companions.

The Bentley, meanwhile, approaches
t from the other end of the scale.
hat it can be made to corner while
olding 1.05g of lateral grip is vastly
npressive, but you're left in little
loubt while you're doing it that
his isn't the GT's finest element.
rushingly able and mildly engaging it
night be, but a sports car it is not.

UYING AND OWNING

★★★★☆

The Continental GT is a generously
quipped car in standard £135k trim
nd, as such, would cost you much
ess in depreciation, over a typical
hree-year ownership, than our test car
night, with its £40,000 of options.

Truth is, you could easily kit out your
GT with must-have extras, such as the
carbon brakes and convenience pack,
and escape the showroom having
spent less than you would on a mid-
spec Ferrari California or Aston Virage.

Our sub-15mpg average economy
return was poor, but balanced against
the GT's immaculate record for
reliability, it could be considered a
small price to pay.

Bentley Continental GT

AUTOCAR VERDICT ★★★★☆

The Continental GT is full of charm and still able to impress

The revisions to the Continental GT run deep but they don't transform the car, so it's a credit to how well it was engineered in the first instance that it still feels so impressive, solid and satisfying.

Few cars have such a mighty powertrain and, although we're disappointed with the fuel economy, there's little denying the pace and flexibility. They go a long way to making the GT supreme at shortening distances.

Complaints? The interior wasn't an ergonomic delight before and little has changed. The ride, too, is not as compliant as its most cosseting rivals'. However, there are a few cars that can get away with such idiosyncrasies and, thanks to a feeling that it's impeccably and individually built, the Continental GT is one of them. It has its failings, yes, but it also has charm.

TESTERS' NOTES

MATT PRIOR
The fuel filler and boot release buttons are worryingly close to the window switches.

MATT SAUNDERS
The dials are superbly visible, even in bright sunlight. The orange is particularly luminous.

VICKY PARROTT
At this money, I'd expe the seats to be cooled a well as heated. They aren't – a hangover of this car architecture's age, I suspect.

JOBS FOR THE FACE

- **Take a few kgs out the bodyshell.**
- **Refine and update interior ergonomics.**
- **Improve the fuel economy.**

AUTOCAR ROAD TEST TOP FIVE

MAKE	FERRARI	ASTON MARTIN	BENTLEY	MASERATI	MERCEDES
Model	**California**	**Virage**	**Continental GT**	**GranTurismo S Auto**	**CL65 AMG**
Price	£146,910	£159,995	£135,760	£88,590	£161,595
Power	453bhp at 7750rpm	489bhp at 6500rpm	567bhp at 6000rpm	434bhp at 7000rpm	621bhp at 4600-5300r
Torque	357lb ft at 5000rpm	420lb ft at 5750rpm	516lb ft at 1700-5400rpm	362lb ft at 4750rpm	737lb ft at 2300-4300r
0-60mph	3.9sec	4.9sec	4.6sec	5.0sec (claimed, to 62mph)	4.4sec (claimed, to 62r
Top speed (claimed)	193mph	186mph	198mph	183mph	155mph (limited)
Fuel economy (combined)	21.6mpg	18.8mpg	17.1mpg	18.6mpg	19.8mpg
Kerb weight (claimed)	1735kg	1890kg	2320kg	1880kg	2240kg
CO_2/tax band	299g/km, 35 per cent	349g/km, 35 per cent	384g/km, 35 per cent	354g/km, 35 per cent	334g/km, 35 per cent
	Highly convincing hybrid of sports car, GT and convertible. Fast, too	**The Bentley's closest spiritual rival. Gorgeous, able and relaxing GT.**	**Brutal cruiser with new-found dynamic edge and refinement; still flawed.**	**Stirring Italian is flawed but not short on charm. And what an engine.**	**German rocketship is special enough for th money. Relaxing, tho**
	★★★★☆	★★★★☆	★★★★☆	★★★☆☆	★★★☆☆

Verdict on every new car page 76

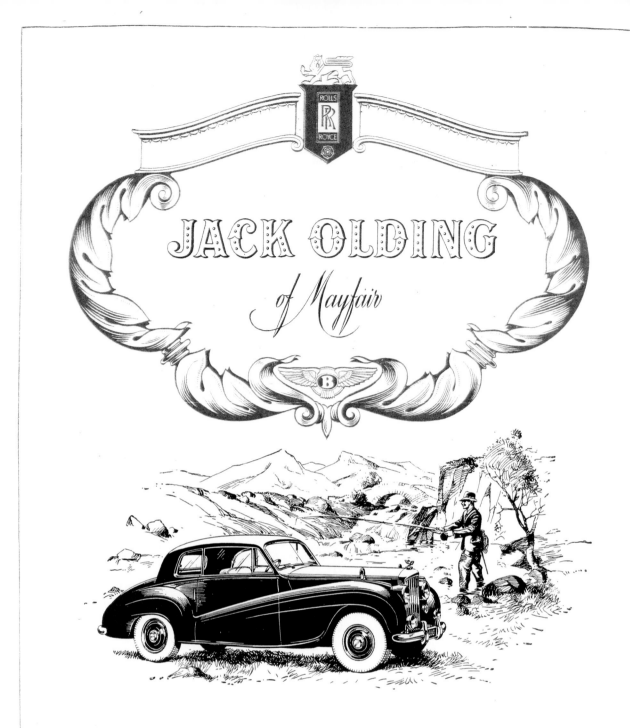

JACK OLDING
of Mayfair

Official Retailer

ROLLS-ROYCE & BENTLEY CARS

Details of New & Used Cars on Application

AUDLEY HOUSE, NORTH AUDLEY STREET LONDON W.1.

Telephone: MAYFAIR 5242-3-4

K/JO. 21